**Enriching the primary curriculum: child, teacher, context**

**Series editor: Janet Moyles**

The series highlights some of the major challenges and issues which face teachers on a day-to-day basis in handling their apparently ever widening roles in primary schools. Curriculum experiences can, and should be enriching and stimulating for everyone but there must be a recognition and appreciation of the crucial interface between child, teacher and the context of school and society, rather than a focus on mere curriculum 'delivery'.

Each volume in the series seeks to enrich and extend readers' curriculum thinking beyond the current narrow confines through recognizing and celebrating the very essence of what makes primary teaching demanding but exciting, creative, dynamic and, yes, even enjoyable! The series recognizes that at the heart of teaching lies children and that 'subjects' are merely tools towards enabling an education which develops both understanding and enthusiasm for life-long learning.

The authors' underpinning, integrated rationale is to enable teachers to analyse their own practices by exploring those of others through cameos of real life events taken from classroom and school contexts. The aim throughout is to help teachers regain their sense of ownership over changes to classroom and curricular practices and to develop an enhanced and enriched understanding of theory through practice.

*Current and forthcoming titles:*

Florence Beetlestone: *Creative children, imaginative teaching*
Max de Boo: *Enquiring children, challenging teaching*
Deirdre Cook and Helen Finlayson: *Interactive children, constructive teaching*
Roger Merry: *Successful children, successful teaching*
Janet Moyles: *Playful children, inspired teaching*
Wendy Suschitzky and Joy Chapman: *Valued children, informed teaching*
Jill Williams: *Independent children, sensitive teaching*

# VALUED CHILDREN, INFORMED TEACHING

## Wendy Suschitzky
### and Joy Chapman

**Open University Press**
Buckingham • Philadelphia

Open University Press
Celtic Court
22 Ballmoor
Buckingham
MK18 1XW

email: enquiries@openup.co.UK
world wide web: http://www.openup.co.UK

and

325 Chestnut Street
Philadelphia, PA 19106, USA

First Published 1998

A catalogue record of this book is available from the British Library

ISBN   0 335 19794 9 (hb)    0 335 19793 0 (pb)

*Library of Congress Cataloging-in-Publication Data*
Suschitzky, Wendy, 1946–
    Valued children, informed teaching/by Wendy Suschitzky and Joy Chapman.
    p.   cm. – (Enriching the primary curriculum – child, teacher, context)
    Includes bibliographical references (p. ) and index.
    ISBN 0-335-19794-9 (hardcover). – ISBN 0-335-19739-0 (pbk.)
    1. Education, Elementary – Great Britain.   2. Elementary school teaching – Great Britain.   3. Educational equalization – Great Britain.
4. Multicultural education – Great Britain.   5. Classroom environment – Great Britain.   I. Chapman, Joy, 1937– .   II. Title.   III. Series.
LA633.S87   1998
372.941–dc21                                                                     98–9208
                                                                                          CIP

Typeset by Graphicraft Typesetters Ltd, Hong Kong
Printed in Great Britain by St Edmundsbury Press Ltd,
Bury St Edmunds, Suffolk

# Contents

# Series editor's preface

## Cameo

Glenn has taught across the age range in different primary schools for the last 15 years, specializing in art. In that time, he has had to make many adjustments in his thinking. The emphasis now appears to have shifted significantly from considering the learning needs of children as paramount, to 'delivering' a curriculum over which he feels little ownership and about which he feels even less real enthusiasm! The National Curriculum with its individual subjects and language of 'teaching', not to mention an impending Office for Standards in Education (Ofsted) inspection, has shaken his confidence somewhat in his own understanding of what primary education is all about. It has also meant that he feels *he* is doing most of the learning, rather than the children – all those detailed plans and topic packs for individual subjects which teachers have been developing within the school seem to Glenn to leave little for children to actually do except explore the occasional artefact and fill in worksheets.

Yet he knows that he enjoys the 'buzz' of teaching, revels in being part of children's progress and achievements, delights in those rare times when he can indulge in art activities with children, is appreciated by parents and colleagues for the quality of his work and, generally, still finds his real heart lies in being an educator and doing something worthwhile. His constant question to himself is 'How can I work with children in ways I feel and *know* are appropriate and yet meet the outside demands made on me?'

Sound familiar? You may well begin to recognize a 'Glenn' within you! He encapsulates the way many teachers are feeling at the present time and the persistent doubts and uncertainties which continually underpin many teachers' work. In the early and middle years of primary schooling in particular, teachers are facing great challenges in conceiving how best to accommodate the learning needs of children in a context of growing pressure, innovation and subject curriculum demand. Yet conscientiousness drives the professional to strive for greater understanding – that little bit more knowledge or skill might just make a big difference to one child, or it might provide improved insights into one aspect of the curriculum.

Glenn, like many teachers, needs time, encouragement and support to reflect on his current practice and to consider in an objective way the changes needed. Rather than trying to add something else to an already overcrowded curriculum, today's teachers should consider those existing aspects which are fundamental to ensuring that children are not only schooled but educated in the broadest possible sense. Only then can we begin to sort out those things which are vital, those things we would like to do, and those things which would benefit from a rethink.

This series aims to offer practitioners food for thought as well as practical and theoretical support in establishing, defining and refining their own understandings and beliefs. It focuses particularly on enriching curriculum experiences for everyone through recognizing and appreciating the crucial interface between the child, the teacher and the context of primary education, including the curriculum context. Each title in the series seeks collectively and individually to enhance teachers' understanding about the theories which underpin, guide and enrich quality practice in a range of broader curriculum aspects, whilst acknowledging issues such as class size and overload, common across primary schools today.

Each book operates from the basis of exploring teachers' sound – frequently intuitive – experiences and understanding of teaching and learning processes and outcomes which most teachers inevitably possess in good measure and which, like Glenn, they often feel constrained to use. For example, the editor is regularly told by teachers and others in primary schools that they 'know' or 'feel' that play for children is or must be a valuable process, yet they are also aware that this is not often reflected in their planning or curriculum management and that the context of education generally is antithetical to play. What is more, they really do not know what to do about it and find articulating the justification for play practices extremely difficult. Other writers in the series have suggested that this is also the case in their areas of expertise.

All the books in this series seek to enrich and extend teachers' curriculum thinking beyond the level of just 'subjects', into dimensions related to the teaching and learning needs of children and the contextual demands faced by schools. The books cover areas such as creativity, success and competence, exploration and problem solving, information technology across subjects and boundaries, play in the primary curriculum, questioning and teacher–child interactions, values in relation to equality issues, social, moral and spiritual frameworks and physical aspects of teaching and learning. Each book has had, within its working title, the rationale of the unique triad of child, teacher and context which underpins all primary schooling and education, for example in this particular case, valued children and informed teaching. This has served to emphasize for authors the inextricable and imperative balance in this triad for effective classroom and curriculum practices. The model we have developed and agreed is shown below.

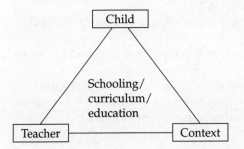

All the writers in the series have been concerned to emphasize the quality, nature and extent of existing classroom practices, and how it is possible to build on these sound pedagogical bases. For this reason, chapters within each title often begin with two or more cameos offering features of practice as starting points for teasing out aspects requiring enquiry, analysis, evaluation and discussion. Chapters then develop their own relevant themes but with consistent reference to what these mean to children and teachers within the general autonomy, and constraints, of the school context.

Issues concerning the *child* take their stance from cognitive psychology and include the child as:

- an active searcher after meaning;
- an individual with particular perceptions of the world and their part in it;
- a person who can reflect on their own learning and understanding;
- a learner with his or her own curriculum needs and interests to be considered;
- an interactive person, learning in collaboration with peers and adults;
- a unique individual but also one with collective needs;
- a member of a 'social' community, i.e. home, family, school, wider community.

Aspects to do with the teaching role lay stress on the *teacher* as a reflective and critical professional who will occasionally but regularly need to stand back from day-to-day practice in order to think about and analyse the triadic relationships and to acknowledge:

- their own learning styles and experiences;
- their own beliefs, values, knowledge and conceptual understanding of pedagogy;
- their need to raise questions about practice and find solutions in an ongoing way;
- their role as mutual learners with children and colleagues;
- their responsibilities as facilitators of learning, as models of learning and as negotiators of meaning with children;
- their role in enabling children's learning rather than always in 'teaching';
- their function as observers and assessors of children's understandings as well as outcomes;
- their obligation clearly to conceptualize the whole curriculum of which the National Curriculum is a part.

When we consider the *context* of pedagogy, this focus subsumes such aspects as the learning environment, school ethos and the actual classroom and school. It also includes such elements as:

- the physical environment – indoors and outdoors;
- the social environment of school and schooling (e.g. is the child an outcome of the context or has the context influenced the child?);
- the psychological environment of school and schooling;
- the philosophical considerations within schools and aspects such as teachers' beliefs and values;
- the curriculum context, including the National Curriculum where this is relevant and appropriate, but also showing where this does not necessarily meet pedagogical needs;
- the frameworks within which the whole concept of schooling takes place and where this fits education in a broader sense.

The overall rationale for each book in the series starts from a belief that teachers should be enabled to analyse their own practices in specific aspects of the broader curriculum as a major aspect of their professionalism. The books are particularly useful at a time of continual curriculum change, when reflection is being focused back upon the child and pedagogy generally as the only perpetuating and consistent elements.

As an integral component, all the books weave teachers' assessment of children's learning and understanding into each particular focus, the intention being to show how the planning>learning >assessment>planning cycle is vital to the quality and success of children's and teachers' learning experiences. With their practical ideas, challenges and direct relevance to classroom practice, these books offer ways of establishing theory as *the* adjunct to practice; they build on teachers' thinking about how they already operate such approaches in the classroom and help teachers to consider how they may enrich, extend and advance their practices to the mutual benefit of themselves, the children, the curriculum and education in society as a whole.

*Valued Children, Informed Teaching* is concerned with all those aspects which, as the authors point out, are often 'put away in the cupboard 'til home time' along with the various artefacts children bring to school as extensions of their life beyond being 'pupils'. In a sensitive and perceptive way, Wendy Suschitzky and Joy Chapman explore with readers the many aspects of children's and teachers' lives which, although seemingly peripheral to meeting curriculum demands, have a determining impact on learning and teaching in all primary schools. Whatever the cultural, political and community context, all schools evolve their own ethos which needs its underpinnings openly and honestly explored to ensure that everyone's most valued mores and 'possessions' are heeded and held in high esteem.

Using this unique idea of storing away 'valuables' in the well-known classroom cupboard, the authors show what diversity of 'possessions' may sometimes be inappropriately stowed away when they should be left out in full view, and in the clear knowledge that they are issues with significant pedagogical implications which are sometimes not supported by the political context.

Our diverse possessions are many and come as part of everyone's personal 'baggage'. In this book, readers are encouraged not only to answer questions but to know which ones they should raise to inform practice in values education. For example, which are the most notable aspects of themselves and their lives brought by children and teachers to the school context? How do our belief systems as teachers affect our teaching styles? How do teachers and children find out about each other's identity? How can children be helped to value each other's background cultures and variations in lifestyles? How do we establish respect for diversity and difference in schools? What exactly are we communicating to children about our values as we go about our day-to-day work in the classroom? These and many other questions are probed throughout this book in which Wendy and Joy offer a significant, new and inspiring contribution to our understanding of the ways in which all these aspects impinge on successful education within differentiated practices for primary age children.

This is not just another book about equality issues: it is much more. Drawing as they do on a whole range of issues – from individual identity and what makes a person unique; language diversity and communication; the essential ingredients for developing learning relationships across age, gender, physical ability, class, geography and culture; through to home and community issues – Joy and Wendy offer their own considered and substantive views on all those aspects to which teachers must attend if they are to provide fully and effectively for the all-round education of each and every child for whom they are responsible.

For those many teachers who find such aspects as differentiation and diversity particularly challenging, this book will offer enormous support and encouragement in evaluating and reviewing many aspects of practice. Ways of counteracting some of the inevitable dilemmas to be found within some contexts are openly and thoughtfully examined and equitable ways forward are explored. Practical ideas supported with strong theoretical underpinnings are presented to show how the effects of informed teaching express values to children which impact upon their own views of self and individual capabilities. Through a range of thoughtful and expressive cameos, each chapter challenges teachers to reflect on their own values, thinking and practices in order to enrich and extend existing curriculum experiences for children with due regard to the communities whose future they represent. Activities are provided so that teachers can relate ideas directly to their own school's practices and, at a variety of levels, probe ever more deeply into their own beliefs as a foundation for successful teaching and learning.

Readers will quickly recognize Wendy's and Joy's own deep commitment to aspects of multicultural education which, using their own definition, is much broader than generally perceived and is about realizing an education for all children in which ultimately they will reach their full, individual potential within the whole curriculum. Their powerful argument will leave few readers in any doubt about each individual child's and teacher's right to have all their implicit but valuable 'possessions' accessible and 'brightly displayed' (as Joy and Wendy put it) in celebration not only of their uniqueness but of their diversity. The concepts inherent within *Valued Children, Informed Teaching* certainly offer a veritable store-house (or is it a classroom cupboard?) of ideas and information for enriching the primary curriculum for everyone.

*Janet Moyles*

# Acknowledgements

We would like to express our thanks to all those colleagues and children who, over many years in primary and community education, have provided the contexts for our cameos and have been the catalyst for our thinking. We would like to acknowledge the invaluable learning that we have gained through working with members of diverse communities, who have shared their cultures, beliefs, ideas and experiences with us.

Sincere thanks go to our editor, Janet Moyles, for her professional expertise and unfailing support, which has enabled this book to be possible.

Special thanks to Neil Byrne for his expert help with preparing parts of the manuscript.

# Introduction

Let us begin by telling you a story about a primary school.

**Cameo**

The teachers and support staff at St Everybody's Primary
School have been lobbying the senior management team for
some time to provide them with a new central store cupboard.
Eventually the headteacher sends round the following Memo:

> In order to persuade the Governor's Finance Committee
> to authorize payment on a new storage facility, I need to
> present a detailed and well argued case. Please discuss
> the following questions and send comments by the next
> management meeting.
>
> 1 Which resources are so important that they must be
>   kept in a special store?
> 2 Why are these items more special than others?
> 3 How should they be stored?
> 4 Who will have access to them?
> 5 Who will be responsible for them?

In trying to answer these questions, it was very soon apparent
that the headteacher had underestimated the depth of
discussion that was needed to arrive at any consensus from
the staff, which consisted of twelve female and two male
teachers of varied ages and backgrounds. The support staff,
female with one male, were also from a wide spectrum of our
multi-ethnic society. Each question raised fundamental issues
related to individual and collective attitudes and experience.

The first question concerns items that each person considers are valuable and so in need of protection in a safe place. As the staff discussed this question, it was apparent that there was immediate agreement on certain items to be stored. However, the list grew and grew as each individual person named an item of special importance to them. The music specialist wanted the brass instruments stored and the premises officer wanted the polishing machine to be in a special place. In order to solve the dilemma, staff were asked to give reasons for the inclusion of items so that a collective response to the second question could be agreed. The main issue being discussed was whether each individual should be allowed to select one or two items or whether only items that had reached a degree of consensus should be stored.

As the staff considered the third question, it was obvious that there was a vast spread of knowledge and experience of storage facilities, in terms of appropriate size, position and construction materials. Individual requests needed to be taken into account such as the height of shelves to consider people's varying physical attributes and labelling would need to take account of the literacy levels of some parents who might use the store.

However, the question of who should have access to the store raised the most heated discussion, with opinions ranging from 'for teachers only' to 'open access to children, staff and parents'. The reasons given to back the various arguments demonstrated each individual's underpinning value system, which reflected their educational philosophy. The final question concerning accountability sparked a deep-seated discussion about the context of primary education and the different levels of responsibility held by teachers, school managers, the local community and central government.

The skill of the senior management team in sustaining relationships and ensuring effective communication of ideas was put to the test. Time was allocated for in depth discussions and a consensus finally reached. The staff found that they now knew more about each other's viewpoints on much wider issues than just storage facilities.

## Value systems

In this book we will examine the obvious and more overt questions raised in this cameo. Children and teachers are the most valuable resources in primary education: we will examine how both can be given true value within the context of primary class-rooms. In Chapter 1, we suggest that the most valuable items to be protected are aspects of an individual's identity. We will describe the elements that make up identity and provide ways to ensure that diverse lifestyles are accorded equal respect. As each person has different characteristics so each school is diverse. The particular aspects that make up the identity of an individual school will also be explored. Like the staff in the cameo, we will decide on what should go into the cupboard but also ask whether children and teachers are required to hide away certain aspects. A frequently heard request to a child, who has brought some potentially unacceptable item into school, is 'Put it in the cup-board until hometime'. We ask whether certain elements of a child's or teacher's identity, such as language or social class, are hidden in the cupboard during the day and only acknowledged after school has closed. The following frequently quoted state-ment from the Bullock Report is still appropriate today:

> No child should be expected to cast off the language and culture of the home as he crosses the school threshold, nor to live and act as though school and home represent two totally separ-ate and different cultures which have to be kept firmly apart.
> (Bullock Report 1975: 286:20.5)

In Chapters 2, 3 and 4, we explore ways to ensure that the valu-able items are stored effectively. The language of equal opportunit-ies is well established in many schools but how teachers respond to diversity is not easily translated into classroom practice. A true learning partnership with children can only be achieved if there is acceptance of what the child brings to the context and an acknowledgement of the teacher's value system. The interaction between child and teacher in all aspects of the primary class-room and the implications for learning will be examined. A warm and trusting relationship between child and teacher and between the other adults in a school are essential ingredients in the provi-sion of high-quality education. We will consider the establishment and maintenance of the learning relationship. In Chapter 3, we acknowledge the importance of valuing different modes of com-munication and of finding shared meanings within the primary environment. Factors that contribute to the creation of a positive climate for children's learning will be explored in Chapter 4. We investigate the role of home and community in Chapter 5, and the access to the primary store cupboard that is accorded to 'the significant others' in children's lives. In Chapter 6, we attempt to answer the final question posed in the cameo of how we protect our 'valuables'. We conclude in the Epilogue by suggesting ways in which a balance can be found between the responsibilities of children, teachers and the context of the wider society.

Our book will examine the issues raised in the cameo, in terms of their importance to primary-aged children and to the teachers who are responsible for their learning together with the wider context of that learning. It is vital to be an informed teacher in an informed teaching context. This book aims to raise teachers' knowledge base about equality issues. It is therefore crucial that practitioners acknowledge the importance of being informed about the social context of their work and engage in the study of the implications of this for their classroom practice. We believe that practitioners do matter and only they can ensure that all children are valued and that the teaching provided is well informed.

The book will embody a holistic approach to equality in primary education with an emphasis on diversity in all its forms. While giving due weight to the educational influences of race and gender, these will not be considered in isolation from influences on other forms of diversity such as physical ability, class and geographical location. The theme of the book is a consideration of the response of teachers to children from varying groups, the response of children to teachers from different backgrounds and the response of schools to both. Cameos will form the backbone of each chapter and will be based on actual events in primary classrooms to which teachers can relate. The book will use a definition of multiculturalism, which encompasses the cultural life of all children in Britain today, whether this is being a wheelchair user, living in a single parent family or in a rural environment. The cameos will reflect these varied contexts. Each chapter will develop the themes established by the cameos and relate these to the three aspects of the child, the teacher and the context. The book aims to change practice by suggesting classroom approaches that are grounded in theory but alert to the realities of the classroom. We hope to achieve this blend of theory and practice by drawing upon our common experiences of working in multi-ethnic contexts and community education and our complementary backgrounds in academic and school-based work.

# 1

# Identity: what is it that makes me *me*?

**Cameo 1**

Amina, a Malaysian child aged 9 years, who is a new arrival in Britain, is working with Mrs Richards, a language support teacher, in a small group situation. It is the beginning of December and there have already been several Christmas preparation activities in the school. The child, a Muslim, is addressing Mrs Richards.

*Amina:* Are you Christmas?
*Mrs Richards:* Do you mean am I a Christian? Yes I am and I celebrate Christmas.

**Cameo 2**

The brown envelope from Ofsted has arrived in a local primary school and staff are discussing preparations for the imminent inspection. Mrs Stace, the deputy head asks:

'Do you think that we should change the pattern of our assemblies? I don't know whether I should continue to do them all on my own so that you can keep the slow readers behind in the classroom to catch up. Perhaps this shouldn't happen and we should be thinking about a more collective type of assembly?'

## Introduction

In this chapter we will describe the items that we consider have a profound influence on the quality of primary education. These are the items which must be valued and stored in the special cupboard, as proposed in the cameo in the Introduction. 'Identity' is how we recognize ourselves and are recognized by others. This recognition is by certain characteristics, which may be individual or may be the same as those belonging to others. Identity formation is a continuing process and as Siraj-Blatchford (1995) suggests, this process in young children is very complex. A child comes to school from home with some sense of an identity already formed. However, security in acceptance of one's own identity can be challenged if the school does not foster a recognition of diversity. We and the children need to understand that identity is made up of many elements, and differences in one or two aspects are a way of establishing that identity. This chapter examines the given elements that make up the identity of a child and, using the same process, examines the identity of a teacher. This process will then be extended to consider the various elements that form the identity of a school.

## Respect for individuals

### Child

Amina is asking Mrs Richards to provide personal information about herself. She is demonstrating a need for knowledge of her teacher's identity for she is aware of a difference between them. Surrounded as she is by images and actions of a culture new to her, she is nevertheless able, through her emerging knowledge of the English language, to construct a fairly meaningful question. The question Amina asks tells us that religion is an important part of her life and she already associates Christmas with being a Christian.

### Teacher

Mrs Richards responds positively. If she had not understood Amina's meaning and asked for repetition or for clarification, this could have undermined the child's confidence and thus affected the relationship. A positive response also sends a powerful message to the other children in the group and helps them to respect the honest enquiry of the new child. The teacher, however, is faced with a dilemma. Should she reply honestly about her religious convictions or only respond in the secular in terms of celebrating a custom? In this scenario, Mrs Richards was able to identify herself as a Christian but non-practising teachers might feel threatened by such an inquiry. How open and honest are we to children about our beliefs? Do we encourage questions or are we vague and fudge our way through in order to soften the edges?

Having been encouraged by a positive response, Amina may have asked the same question of her class teacher but received a totally different response depending upon that individual's personal stance. This will send a message to children that teachers are individuals with different stances also warranting respect. The child therefore has to interpret language and hidden meanings in each new situation.

## Context

The school has provided a support system for this child by giving individual time which allowed such an interaction to take place. The teacher had correctly understood the underlying message in Amina's question and had knowledge of the child's culture. Schools must ensure that staff have this knowledge. There was obviously a climate whereby the child felt confident to ask such a question. The emphasis placed on Christmas in schools certainly needs to be explained to children and parents from other religious backgrounds.

The above cameo has shown that the way that both Amina and Mrs Richards view themselves is an important factor in their work together. In the next section, we will explore how self-concept influences the learning environment in primary schools. Following on from this discussion, we will take each aspect that contributes to a personal identity, and examine the issues that arise for classroom practice. As the staff in the cameo in the Introduction were required to select items of value for special storage, so we will describe the aspects of both a child and a teacher's identity that are to be valued within the context of primary education.

## How do we view ourselves?

The complexity of teaching is acknowledged by the educational establishment (Schmid 1961; Calderhead 1987), and teachers' work is known to be intellectually challenging (Galton 1995). A central part of teaching and learning is the evaluations made as teachers appraise children and children appraise each other and their teachers. The ways that children view themselves are influenced by the ways others respond to them. A person's self concept is made up of two elements: *self-image*, which is descriptive and *self-esteem*, which is evaluative (Merry 1997). The way you describe yourself is your self-image, for example, 'I have brown skin, I am a girl and I am deaf'. Your self-concept is an understanding of yourself which has been formed from the influences exerted from the outside, and this will have an effect on a person's attitude to learning (Lawrence 1996). A good self-concept will not necessarily mean high academic achievement but a poor one may stop people reaching their full potential (Kutnick 1988). Self-concept can play an important part in the recognition or denial of an aspect of identity such as ethnicity (Verma and Mallick 1988).

The relationship between a teacher's self-concept and effective teaching is as important as that between the child's self-concept and effective learning. Burns suggests

> Teachers possess self-concepts which affect their own and the pupils' behaviour, their ability to build sound relationships with the pupils, their style of teaching, and their perceptions and expectations of themselves as teachers and of children as learners.
>
> (Burns 1982: 251)

Hall and Hall (1988) suggest that teachers should be encouraged to have a better awareness of themselves and their own behaviour. Burns (1982: 58) reports on studies showing that teachers with a negative view of themselves had a negative effect on children's achievement.

We need to have knowledge of children's identity in order to have some understanding of their behaviour patterns. The culture that children have experienced will have formed their knowledge of behaviour, speech and relationships and provided understanding of the expectations of family and community. But teachers must use this knowledge with care so as not to make assumptions or perpetuate a stereotype. It should be noted that one can have an extensive knowledge of a cultural pattern of living but still hold a negative stance towards it.

Many characteristics that make up identity are 'givens'. For example, young children do not choose to belong to groupings such as family, gender or locality so these are given rather than chosen. Some categories are more easily definable than others; for example, physical distinctions are easier to describe than social class. But it is not just the description that is important but the terminology used which must not be value-laden. A person described as a 'dwarf' has a recognizable height but the term can also have negative connotations within the social setting.

We have offered reasons for gaining knowledge of children's identity but do children need to have knowledge of their teacher's identity? Should teachers discuss aspects of their personal life with the children in their care? Hall and Hall (1988) suggest that once a relationship has been established, then questions of a personal nature can be answered without difficulty. We would argue that the teacher–child relationship is enhanced by teachers giving greater knowledge of their out-of-school life. Many teachers may feel that this is unnecessary and has no educational advantage. In order to find some evidence for teacher self-disclosure, a small survey was conducted by the authors of 16–19-year olds, who were asked to reflect on their relationship with their primary school teachers. A substantial majority expressed the opinion that a more open teacher improved the teacher–child relationship. Comments included:

'I trusted her more.'

'Teachers who sound "human" are always more popular.'

'I felt more at ease.'

It may be that we need to select certain pieces of personal information to share and others to hide. Dilemmas can be found if the teacher's life is very different from the child's, as shown in cameo 1. Another example would be the teacher who lives in a four-bedroom house trying to empathize with the child who lives in a small flat. What about the teacher from a large, urban family understanding the needs of an only child from a rural background? If teachers can admit to some failing, such as 'I used to hate practising the piano but now I enjoy playing in assembly', this places them on a similar level to the child. If children are not accustomed to knowing first names, ages or religion of their teachers, then this can cause sniggers. Young children frequently believe that the teacher lives in the school and cannot have a 'normal life' so there are few perceived links with the reality of the child's life. An example of successful self-disclosure occurred after a teacher had taken an Eid festival assembly, having identified himself as Muslim. A Muslim boy in another class approached this teacher shaking his hand and saying, with pride, 'I'm a Muslim, too, sir'.

## Elements that contribute to children's and teachers' identity

Although young children are still in the process of forming their identity, the factors that contribute to that identity are the same as those of adults such as the teachers. So for this part of the chapter, when considering key issues, it is difficult to separate the child and the teacher and necessary to explore the educational impact of identity issues for all who are involved in primary schools.

People have multiple identities that impact on one another (Cole 1997) and the significance placed on certain elements will vary from individual to individual. As Gaine (1995) suggests, this will depend on context and how others view the aspect of identity such as skin colour. It is not the aspect of identity itself that is important but how individual people respond. Continually, we have moments of choice when we select which aspects of identity to highlight. The more we have a need to express our identity, the more we will deliberately make certain choices.

Personal identity can be divided into eight areas, which will now be examined in turn.

- Gender.
- Family.
- Abilities.
- Communication.
- Locality.
- Socio-economic factors.
- Culture.
- Physical attributes.

However, we agree with Modood *et al.* (1994) that the boundaries between groups are unclear and can be overlapping or indistinct. It must be emphasized that the relationship between each of the areas is significant (Suschitzky 1995a). The eight defined areas are not all necessarily equal in their impact on discrimination. A person's location may be a cause for discrimination but factors of race or class will have a vastly greater affect. Also people who can be described as being from the same category will perceive themselves in different ways (Siraj-Blatchford 1995). For example, a disabled child from a middle-income family may have very different experiences to one from a family with a low income.

## Gender

A child's perception of his or her gender is not just determined by biology but by the way that society perceives male and female (Oakley 1985). This perception has been formed from experience and has been influenced by others in a social value system. So one child's view of boys may be different from another's but negative inferences may also have been absorbed. One question to ask is whether it matters if the teacher is male or female. Boys may try to devalue female teachers, based on sexist attitudes found at home and so resist female authority. But women teachers may feel that these attitudes are due to their own inadequacies whereas the influence comes from outside school. There is a lack of male role models available to young children as the majority of primary teachers are women. We suggest that all children should experience the range of gender attributes. There may be a mismatch of a child's previous experiences of gender roles with those found in school. For example, a female headteacher in a position of power may be a difficult concept for a child who has been immersed in ideas promoting the female role as a submissive, obedient one. Similarly, children brought up in single-parent families may have little experience of relating to a teacher of the opposite sex from that of their prime carer.

Discussion of sexual orientation is a sensitive area and one that many teachers feel is inappropriate to their professional status. However, if a boy is continually dressing up in female clothes available in a dressing-up box, then challenges to our value systems often occur. We must recognize that the young child will be forming an identity towards one sex or the other and this may be manifested in the child's behaviour at school. In society, the female 'tomboy' is frequently more acceptable than the boy portraying feminine characteristics. Teachers should not be left alone to struggle with these issues but should rather discuss them with colleagues, parents and others.

## Family

Every child is a member of a family but with the variety of patterns of family structure found in our society today, we need to be aware that relationships can be very varied. The prime carer may be grandma, dad, or foster parent and the child may live in an extended family made up of step siblings or several generations living together. Even if family experience is of many foster homes, a perception of family and relationships will have been formed. The family will often be a constant, providing a lasting thread for the child (Alexander 1997). When a child enters school, relationships are not then so individual as she or he becomes a member of a class of thirty or more other children. There will also be contact with children from homes that adopt different patterns and behaviour such as ones that challenge gender stereotypes. Similarly, every teacher brings an experience of family structure that may be equally as varied as those of the children. Within the classroom, the need is to relate the teacher's experience to that of the child.

## Abilities

Another form of categorizing people is by perceptions of their abilities. Available identities in school are frequently those of 'good' or 'naughty' pupil, 'clever' or 'lazy' child, 'fast' or 'slow' reader, good football player or someone awkward at PE (Tiedt and Tiedt 1990). Children exhibit different forms of both physical and verbal abilities in the classroom and we differentiate by our perceptions of those abilities but also by our like or dislike of certain personality characteristics. Teachers, too, have varied levels of abilities and children are astute enough to be very aware of these. Talented teachers in music, art or sport can enhance the work of the whole school and gifted children can readily relate to such teachers and take inspiration from them. But can teachers who excel in something empathize with the failing child? It can be assumed that teachers' experience of academic work will be of achievement but it is not suggested that teachers cannot understand the less able child. At the other end of the spectrum, we could ask whether the reason we do so little about offering individual opportunities to the most able children is our unwillingness to admit that they are perhaps more intelligent than ourselves.

## Communication

People acknowledge their identity by the 'language' that they speak. Society places great significance on the mode of both the spoken and written word and class, region, and even gender can be construed from the accent, vocabulary and manner of delivery. It is children's early experience of modes of communication that shape their understanding of how people express and exchange ideas and their own membership of a communication family. Diverse identities are found in families where members use Braille, British Sign Language, Makaton, computers as language aids or speak languages which originate from overseas or indigenous 'older' languages such as Gaelic or Welsh. It should be acknowledged that children may be emerging bilinguals and have rich experiences of multilingual environments. Their skills and knowledge of communication should be celebrated and extended in the classroom. Teachers' mode of communication will be as varied as that of the children they teach (see Chapter 3 to try a language line and discover your own communication heritage). With such variety it may well be that teacher and child do not share the same first language, local accent or uses of expression or vocabulary. Chapter 3 explores the implications of this in more depth. We must not forget that in our rapidly changing world, the use of information technology is an increasingly important aspect of children's knowledge of communication. Experiences in these fields will be very varied and also need to be taken into account in school.

## Locality

The locality in which children live, whether this is a rural, suburban or inner-city environment provides differing experience which can be brought into the school context such as knowledge of agriculture, wildlife or industrial patterns. A child's locality can also influence the development of social skills such as independence.

For example, a child living in a tower block may have less inde-pendence than the country bred child but may have a wider experience of meeting people from all walks of life. Children's physical experiences may also differ depending on access to open spaces or public or private transport. Modern transport systems and housing patterns mean that primary teachers are no longer the village schoolteacher but frequently live well away from the immediate locality of the school. Teachers may have originated from the same background as the children but likewise many may have no experience of life in the community background of the school.

### Socio-economic factors

Social class is the most commonly referred to aspect of social identity (Marshall *et al.* 1989). Factors that determine social status are complicated and based on historical precedent. Cole (1997: 66) suggests that the use of terms such a 'upper' or 'working class' imply a 'justification of differentiated social class' but the important issue is the relationship between each class. In school, the terms are frequently used to describe a community rather than an individual, but the terms are still very value-laden. The gap between the performance of children from different social classes widens as they progress through the primary school and it was found that whatever the ethnic origin or gender, social class is strongly associated with academic performance (Ofsted 1996a). Adults can change their status by education and career choice but young children are labelled by the one given by their parents. The social class of teachers can be difficult to describe as the level of pay does not always match qualifications and status.

### Culture

Culture can be defined as those features of a way of life which help to define it and make it distinctive. This can include norms of behaviour passed on through generations, shared activities, identity and a set of systems of expectations (Pring 1992). Cul-ture in this sense is not evaluative. Both teachers and children may identify themselves by their religion and often a label is attached to people's specific level of conviction, for example a committed or nominal Christian. It is difficult to separate culture and religion as our cultural life is either historically or actively based on religious rituals and values. However, other aspects have a part such as class, economic level, geographical and physical attributes. A distinctive example of this is the development of a strong and distinctive deaf culture which arises in homes of deaf persons.

Each person is both an individual and part of a culture but the extent of identification with that culture will vary. Children from families who originate from overseas may be strongly encouraged to keep their cultural traditions within their new cultural community. This need to counter the influence of the host culture may be due to the fact that ethnic minorities face discrimination: so that maintaining cultural identity gives strength. On the other hand, families may make different choices such as taking a positive stance to be part of the main culture. There may be a determination to succeed and this can perhaps only be achieved by adopting the outward image of the majority culture. Making stereotypical assumptions about a child's or a teacher's cultural life is a constant pitfall in educational work.

### Physical attributes

There is a tendency to view only the perfect body as the acceptable one and therefore all physical attributes are measured against that ideal. The perfect female is frequently presented as slim, with white skin and blonde hair and the male tall and rugged. So we evaluate our body by comparing how well it matches to this image. Grasz (source unknown) describes the body as text, 'a writing surface on which messages can be inscribed' but messages can be read and interpreted in many ways. So we describe people for example as 'he has no fingers' instead of 'he is a good runner'. One has to read one's own messages or interpretations about one's physical attributes and accept or challenge other people's interpretations. Both teachers and children with minority skin colour may face discrimination, as may teachers and children with physical disability.

As we acknowledged earlier, although we are all made up of these eight elements, the boundaries between these areas of identity overlap. When trying to find commonality between people, we can be accused of labelling people and so creating stereotypes. Gaine (1995) suggests that even with an apparently homogeneous

*We are all in this together*

group, generalizations are difficult and could be construed as, for example, racist. We need to find common bonds that bring us together and also give us a sense of belonging to a group. But as already stated, not everyone from a recognizable group has the same experiences, feelings or views. We need to acknowledge the individual that is inside the outer shell of the group.

To return to our Cameo in the Introduction (page 1), we all protect things that we value and one way to do this is to place them in a safety deposit box. Two situations can result; one is they may be hidden away forever and the other is that they are kept for special occasions. In every culture, special occasions provide opportunities for dressing up, performing rituals and perhaps taking part in ceremonies. These are the times when we take out the items from the safe deposit box for a while and enjoy them. But the security in some way comes from knowing that they are going to be put away again, not to interfere with daily living. The situation allows the individual the choice of whether to open the box or not. On special occasions, freedom of choice can operate but in everyday life such a freedom may not exist. An acknowledgement of an individual's identity is crucial for the well-being of that person but when looking at educational institutions then conformity is frequently required. The reality for the individual

is that the school can recognize ethnic roots on the special occasions, for example the celebrations held for Diwali, but perhaps
not when studying National Curriculum history, where the topics
taught do not reflect all children's roots.

## What's in a name?

We cannot write a chapter entitled 'Identity' without some reference to names. Both given or chosen first names and surnames
express identity. Surnames can identify our family, country of
origin, language or religion. First names equally do this but
gender, age, and social class can also be identified. On hearing
a person's name, one often forms a mental image, which can be
evaluative and prejudge our relationship with that person. Because names are so personal and say so much about us, many
people choose to make changes or even select a new name. It is
important to learn the correct pronunciation of names and to
challenge teasing and racial abuse. So the name of a person can
be a means of learning about their identity. We all know the
name of the school, but how do we recognize the school's identity? Location and religious attachment are immediately identi-
fiable but the factors that make up the underlying ethos is the
most important. So what are the aspects of identity that are found
in schools?

## Recognizing the identity of a school
*Child*

Upon first reading, it would appear that the child is not present
in Cameo 2 and that matters concerning policy and administra-
tion are the main concerns of the teachers. However, it would be
a glaring error to continue that line of thought for all policy
decisions and administrative directives have a direct bearing upon
the pattern of each individual child's school day. This is true
whether it is the chair upon which a child sits, the manner of
teaching or the time at which children eat dinner. The whole is
made up of innumerable small items all of which define the total
picture. In this cameo, the school has given thought to an aspect
of its reading programme but the desirability or otherwise of
using assembly time will be defined probably by people not

involved in the direct daily running of the school and certainly not someone particularly familiar with its personal requirements. The aspect of the child's identity that is particularly present here is the recognition that, if there is a specific need, a child has a right for that need to be met effectively. Although the school must operate as a working unit it is nevertheless made up of individuals with different needs. Each child within the school must be given the opportunity to develop to the limit of his or her potential using whatever means are most appropriate. However, it must be queried whether the policy of using assembly time for extra work allows equal opportunities for pupils who are reluctant readers.

*Teacher*

In this short communication, the deputy head reveals the dichotomy experienced by so many teachers in schools. No matter how professional careers may develop or how promotion alters status, the original baseline is still one that encompasses identity, initial training and the growth of experience and skills. Promotion, however, places the teacher in a somewhat different role, for with it comes responsibilities and expectations.

Who defines these responsibilities and expectations? Undoubtedly the first definition of them may come from the individual teacher, who will have an image of how best to fulfil the new role. Accompanying that image will be the role as defined by colleagues and authorities to whom they must be accountable and with whom they must work. The term 'accountable' is much overused in many contexts in our current age but it influences the situation heavily and for many teachers may bring a feeling of stress.

So what of the implications of these two aspects of the teacher as shown in this Cameo? Obviously there has been some agreement reached between staff in the school upon strategies that will be most helpful to those children who are experiencing difficulties with reading proficiency. One of these strategies is to try to give them some quality time when the majority of the school is in assembly. This policy decision may not have been unanimously agreed by all staff. Differing opinions may have encompassed views concerning the importance and value of collective worship and religious education for all.

However, the imminent arrival of Ofsted inspectors puts a different light upon many things, not least being their possible attitudes towards the importance of all school pupils being present at acts of collective worship. The deputy head has a responsibility to the needs of staff and children and to the requirements of government legislation. This is where two accountabilities can conflict. The identity of the deputy head in this context is undoubtedly a double one at least. She is a fully trained, competent teacher capable of identifying a child's needs and responding to them sensitively but she is also a member of the senior management team within the school and, as such, must make suitable responses to the requirements of 'officialdom'. However, other aspects of her identity also emerge. She has been part of the negotiation process with members of staff to set up this reading strategy and is still using those skills to discuss the appropriate action to be taken in the approaching inspection. She must make a choice about which identity must take priority in this situation. We are not sure if it will be the competent teacher or the responsible member of the senior management team. She may be guided by the opinions of the staff or make a decision alone.

*Context*

The obvious and immediate context is naturally that of the school. The school as an institution needs to be operating effectively and efficiently for both pupils and staff. It is certainly taking the special needs of some children on board and addressing them in a positive manner. Time and tuition are provided for those children during a period when other factors need not intrude. Similarly, it provides staff with an opportunity for a quiet slot of time in what will undoubtedly be a hectic day. But, of course, the school itself is not operating in isolation. It is one unit in a much larger sphere and its performance is viewed in relation to that of other local schools and indeed to schools across the whole of the country. Thus the Ofsted inspection will produce a report that will indicate at what point on a scale of excellence the school can be placed in relation to other schools. There will be repercussions as a result of the report and in order for the work of the school to progress smoothly it is imperative that the report is capable of being viewed favourably by parents, governors and the local education authority. We have to ask the question: 'To what extent can the school continue working policies it has already approved if there is a possibility of these being at variance with official views?'

Over a period of time, a school ethos will have been formed as a result of a wide variety of factors. There will be times of decision when the school will consider which of these factors must override others. It is just such a situation as presented in cameo 2 that forces such moments of decision.

There are elements that we consider are vital aspects of a school's identity and we explore how these have evolved in individual settings.

## Identity issues for the school

The context of the interaction between child and teacher is the school and this does not provide a neutral environment. As Verma (1988: 7) states, 'an educational system does not exist in a historical and social vacuum'. Likewise, each school cannot exist in a vacuum but is made up of specific attitudes, values and norms of behaviour. The crucial question is how these are determined and whether the influences are from within or imposed from outside.

Using the same process to define school identity as that used to examine children and teachers' identity profiles, we define five elements that we suggest all schools have in common:

- Children and their community.
- Education ethos.
- Participating adults.
- Outside influences.
- Physical factors.

Because diversity lies within these factors, their manifestation makes up the school's individual identity. As with people it is the relationship between the aspects of identity that is important.

### Children and their community

Each school's particular identity is founded upon its children. They will be described by the categories already given for personal identity such as class or culture as will the community in which they live. A school is outside the community by the nature of its official status and yet it is part of the life of the community and is influenced by (the factors of) that community. In Chapter 5 we examine in greater depth the partnership that should develop between a school and the local community.

*Educational ethos*

The educational ethos of a particular school depends upon the teaching styles used, pedagogy, a specific uniform, routines, learned patterns of behaviour, expectations, discipline, the hidden curriculum, self-esteem enhancement, commitment to equal opportunities and many more contributory factors. Alexander (1996: 285) suggests that teachers construct a learning environment that is consistent with their values and translate these into meaningful learning for children. In Chapter 6, we explore ways of finding a common educational ethos that translates into effective primary education.

It is necessary to examine each item of the elements that contribute to the ethos of a school in considerable depth to understand fully the purposes and implications that underlie each one. We provide an example of one below and you might like to take time to explore the others further.

What exactly is understood by the word 'discipline'. Questions that can be raised are:

Are the rules to be obeyed without questioning?
Are the rules to be understood and agreed by all?
Are the reasons for punishments clearly understood by children and staff?
How can consensus be achieved if differing values and codes of behaviour operate?
Do the children have any 'say' in making the rules?

*Participating adults*

Many different adults form part of the school community and their roles, commitments and influence are varied. Who are they in your school? What are the implications of the number of adults and length of service; the language, gender and racial balance of staff; the deployment of support staff; the personal stance of individuals and collective needs? The decisions and the actions of these adults provide a structure for the children but the response of the children influences their effectiveness. The management structure is a most significant influence. It can be examined in terms of team work, collaborative decision making, framework of communication, power structure and policy making. Decisions may be taken in meetings or outside, before or after. The defining of each of these factors needs to be carried out in depth to gain an understanding of the school context.

## Outside influences

Every school has certain statutory duties and since the Education Reform Act 1988 these have been strengthened. National Curriculum, Ofsted inspections and local management of schools have all changed practice in primary schools. What will you teach? How will you teach it? How is it monitored? How is it paid for? The answers to these questions come from central government and to a lesser extent the local education authority. Influences on teaching and learning also come from research, Initial Teacher Training institutions and professional teaching bodies. Other issues need to be raised concerning who trains the teachers and carries out professional development and how access to professional development is controlled within each school.

## Physical factors

The physical environment of a school is crucial for the well-being of all users of the building and the effectiveness of teaching and learning. Age and state of repair of buildings, amount of available space, furnishings, outside environment communal areas and community facilities are all crucial factors. The important issue is what uses are made of the school environment. Who designed the physical environment? The educational ethos at the time of construction also influences the design, such as open plan classrooms, and may need adaptation when ideas change.

---

**ACTIVITY 1.1**

**Identity of a school**

Spend a few minutes thinking of the most significant elements that make up a school that you know well. To each of the aspects of a school's identity that we have suggested, you will be able to add many more.

In fact, what is absent from a school is of as much importance as that which is present. It is important to take a step back from the day-to-day business of teaching and reflect on the identity of our children, the identity of our school and our personal identity and what the relationship between these three mean to teaching and learning.

**STRATEGIES**

**How do teachers discover a child's identity?**

We would suggest that there is a need to collate as much information as possible about the child's identity, but the question must be raised as to how teachers can achieve this amidst the hustle and bustle of what is already an extremely busy career. Rather than suggesting that we should produce yet another confusing form with which to grapple or embark upon a further project, the solution lies in a method of working during the daily running of the general school day. Therefore it does not require any sweeping changes but small adjustments to procedures already in place. Strategies are through:

- Communications.
- Observation.
- Records.
- Curriculum.

*Communications*

Let us start then with the essence of everyday relationships. Talking and listening form a major part of our communications with each other no matter where we are or what we may be doing. In fact, it is such a natural part of our daily lives that usually we may give it little thought at all. But it forms a crucial part of our day. How may we best utilise it to form a picture of a child's identity? The first thing for teachers is to value communication, to give it prominence, and to learn both how to listen to others properly and respond sensitively. This will mean that conversations casually undertaken are nevertheless of importance. Furthermore, the basic curriculum work and the indications of factors forming the child's individual identity will often be inextricably interwoven so that the teacher is forming a picture of both at the same time. A child spends a large part of its days in what at first appears incidental chat but is actually an expression of important facets of his or her individuality. Similarly, conversations which take place with parents during events at the school, or when a home–school liaison worker is talking with them, will obviously reveal aspects of the child's family and community environment which will help teachers to understand the responses of the child.

Home–school links can take a variety of forms from those planned and official, right through to unexpected links and informal contact. To some extent both ends of that spectrum are probably present during the first contacts made between school and home. The issue of home visiting needs to be addressed as a school policy by the management. This will be further explored in Chapter 5. Visitors need to be aware of their personal image and that they are the ambassador for the school and also must be able to relate to the identity of the child and family. Home–school visitors need training to enable them to be fully aware of the implications of their own responses.

*Observation*

Another area whereby teachers may so easily glean information is by developing what is already a well-defined skill for many. That is observation. Many teachers already use this art on a daily basis. All that is needed now is to develop this skill a little further by increasing the quantity of time spent by perhaps two or three minutes and determining a focus for observation. You also need some 'thinking' time in order to plan and anticipate as far as that is possible. The result will be a valuable piece of observation. When that is done, do not lose it! Record it. Obviously it will not be possible to do this for all of the children all of the time. So it will need to be spread as evenly as possible. But over a period of time, it is amazing how profiles of children can thus be compiled.

Profiling is, of course, a specific and sophisticated skill which has been well researched and documented (Ritchie 1991). It is best at first to make an uncomplicated start here by observing a few aspects, and then progressing steadily to a more reflective and concentrated approach. Thus you will move towards a continuous profile of the child which will be of some considerable worth. This will be explored further in Chapter 5.

*Records*

If records are kept short, focused, user-friendly and easily access-ible, then they can prove to be invaluable. They do not need to be records of scholastic achievements only as they will then merely record a small portion of that individual's profile. Indeed, the word 'profile' is a crucial one. Records should give an indication of all aspects of the individual concerned. It would be impossible for one teacher to achieve such a record. Therefore, records held of previous years in the child's development need to be included and added to all the time. Thus a continuous profile will be produced to which new revelations of the child's identity can be added. Recording should be as objective as possible bearing in mind one's own value system and the possible effect on this of one's observations. Try to establish a method of recording 'can do' statements rather than more negative notes.

*Curriculum*

There are many areas and projects which lend themselves to the celebration of individual identity. Familiar topics which spring instantly to mind are 'myself', 'my family' and 'my house'. All that most teachers will have to do in order to find more of the child's identity will be to expand the list of topics to include such things as pastimes, holidays, diet and roles of family members. Then add to this greater opportunities for the children to express themselves in oracy, written and pictorial ways. Oracy plays a major role here. Children should be given a large number of open-ings to talk to each other in group and paired situations and to explain to the larger class group what their written and pictorial work is about. They thus share with each other their identity and enable the teacher to form a true picture of it.

Such identity acknowledgement will be echoed by the resource materials and the curriculum matter which is used within the school. Books and wall displays will reflect the identities of all members and lead the children to recognize identities with which they may be less familiar but which are just as valid. Curric-ulum materials will be chosen carefully to enable children to use their own identity as starting blocks from which to explore the unfamiliar.

In these early years, the children will be positively encouraged to present their work in both written and pictorial forms reflecting

their personal views before moving towards a more sophisticated objective stance. In an environment encouraging such an
honest exchange, teachers should also feel free to participate honestly thereby contributing and receiving as much as the children
themselves. Those teachers who have experienced the warmth of
such opportunities feel sufficiently secure to be open with their
pupils.

Talk and listen + Observe + Record + Curriculum opportunities = Finding a child's identity

---

**STRATEGIES**

**How do children discover a teacher's identity?**

Teachers have an explicit need to find out about the children in
their care, by using the ways suggested above. But for children,
the ways of discovery about teachers are more implicit. They
look, listen, compare and gradually form an image which is
constantly reforming. They make comparisons with known people
and settings beginning with their family then further afield. As
experience widens, so children develop a set of criteria to make
value judgements about people's identity. These are based on that
experience but also are influenced by the home, school and values
presented by the media.

---

## Conclusion

We would agree with Woods (1990) who suggests that a school
should be a trading place, where experiences, knowledge and
skills can be exchanged. The differences of its members should
be acknowledged and catered for. We need to recognize that every
child, every teacher and every school is special and that each
has its own identity. An honest exchange between children and
teachers on a daily basis will form a foundation which is secure.
It will involve recognition by both, of the credibility of the experiences and feelings of the other. This mutual exchange will indicate
that it is both acceptable and desirable to do this. With such honest
recognition, there will easily follow opportunities to celebrate and
share any specific knowledge or skills which an individual may

have. Full use of these aptitudes within the school community will enhance the self-concept of the people concerned and enable others to value what other individuals are able to bring to the situation.

All those engaged in education need to recognize the need to challenge negative views held about aspects of identity and to encourage positive self-images. In order for a caring and stimulating environment to be created, children need to find commonalities with other children and teachers need to find common bonds with other teachers. Both need to find ways to share and celebrate aspects of their individual identities to establish a unique identity of a learning school. In this way, a child or a teacher may find that it is less necessary to hide away in the cupboard one or more aspects of themselves.

Having gained knowledge about each other, how do children and teachers use this information when establishing and maintaining a relationship? Just having some background knowledge about another person is not sufficient in itself to create a good relationship. We can acquire a vast amount of information but may still perceive someone in a negative way. In fact, if the knowledge conflicts with our value systems, then it may be the cause of the low opinion. Chapter 2 will examine the complexity of *relationships* in the primary school and how we can create a positive environment for children's learning.

## 2

# Relationships: building bridges and how to cross them

**Cameo 1**

A primary school class full of eager 9-year-olds is engaged in following a National Curriculum Science module in which the initial stages of electrical circuits are being taught. The activities enable the pupils to perform simple tasks to complete a circuit, which is then proven when small bulbs light up. In the class is Edward, a traveller child from a showman's family. The family has been part of the local area for generations and owns a large fairground ride plus smaller sideshows. Edward has been an active member of his family's work team since he was very young and has progressed from simple work tasks to the more complicated and responsible. A normal everyday part of the workload is to check that all light bulbs on the ride and sideshows are fully operational. This naturally involves a rather large number of lights. He has been nurtured in an environment where he has built up a considerable knowledge of electrical circuits and has a healthy respect for the possible dangers in working with electricity. Therefore, upon being presented with this National Curriculum task, he feels insulted. He responds by firmly folding his arms and refusing to work with the children in his group.

**Cameo 2**

Mr Brown is on playground duty and is deliberately trying to engage Darren, a rather withdrawn Year 2 child, in conversation.

*Mr Brown:*  Is that a new coat?
*Darren:*  Yes, sir.

| Mr Brown: | Where did you get it from? |
|---|---|
| Darren: | The market, sir. |
| Mr Brown: | Who bought it for you? |
| Darren: | My new dad, sir. |
| Mr Brown: | Your coat's a lovely colour. |

The pair continue to walk around the playground without any further conversation between them.

## Introduction

This chapter will examine how teachers and children respond to the knowledge gained about each other and the consequent relationship that is established. A relationship occurs when two people are connected by circumstances. This can be as family members or friends, acquaintances, work colleagues or in official settings. Some of the relationships suggested are established by choice but we do not choose our family members and there is very little choice in connections made in professional circumstances. Similarly, there is usually little choice between a teacher and a child working together in a close setting. However, there are options in the way that the relationship develops by the manner in which we react to others, both internally and overtly, and in our resultant behaviour. It is the quality of these interactions that is vitally important.

In Chapter 1, we looked at ways of obtaining knowledge about each other. However, it is in the formation of a relationship that this knowledge is used in an individual manner by each partner and so determines the nature of the relationship. In this chapter, we will examine the factors that we consider influence the establishment and maintenance of relationships.

Every relationship takes place within a context and this can greatly affect its outcome. Cummins (1996) states that the nature of the personal interactions that occur between teachers and children are central in reversing patterns of underachievement among minority pupils. We will consider this in the context of the primary classroom and the varied relationships found there. We will include the day-to-day interactions between child and teacher but also child with child and between the various adults who work in the school.

## Establishing relationships by acknowledging diversity

### Child

In Cameo 1 it is quite probable that Edward's school attendance has, of necessity, been interrupted. There will be times when it is easy for him to attend but others where it is difficult or even impossible depending upon the particular travel patterns of his family. It is likely that there is a regular winter base where his family live, followed by a touring itinerary that may vary only a little from year to year. It is this mobility that will dictate his pattern of education: there will probably be a 'winter' school where he is well known and other schools around the country to which he and his family will feel far less committed. This cultural pattern will greatly influence his attitude to learning in general. In theory, there may well be a family desire for a firm commitment to the child's schooling but in practice the demands of the family business will probably be the stronger force diluting this commitment.

It therefore follows that Edward's attendance at school may not be totally willing and he would probably prefer to be helping to paint and refurbish the rides and shows for the coming season. To be confronted by work well below his ability will only antagonize him further and make him more reluctant to attend school. He will feel that his previous knowledge has been completely ignored. The relationship with his teacher will come under great strain and there may be a loss of respect for her. His willingness to cooperate in other timetable subjects may also be questionable.

### Teacher

How is the teacher to react in such a situation? It may well be an unexpected dilemma. For someone to whom the traveller culture is a new experience, it may be both confusing and infuriating. For others who have some knowledge of the background, it may still present something of a challenge. If the child does not cooperate, the authority of the teacher will be threatened and may be copied by other members of the class, thus undermining the whole ethos of the smoothly operating classroom. The teacher may well feel that her professional adequacy is being questioned. Moreover, there are tick lists to be completed for each child to show

that they have performed, understood and applied the requirements of the science curriculum.

The effect on the teacher–child relationship can be significant.
If a rapport has already been established with the child, it may
be possible to talk the child through the learning and either come
to some agreement or find alternative appropriate work. This, of
course, will depend upon the quantity of staff and time available.
Because it has been an unexpected situation, it is unlikely that there
will have been the opportunity to be prepared for it. If support
staff for traveller children have already been part of the liaison, it
may well be that the situation can be resolved fairly easily. But
all of this will necessarily be dependent upon the teacher's initial
response to receiving a traveller child into her class. This in turn
is dependent upon her own personal stance on issues of diversity. If she feels the child's behaviour is a threat, then her response
will be more negative towards the child. However if she is secure
in her viewpoint, then she will accept the child's statement and
be able to accommodate it. Should there be a breakdown in the
relationship then the intended learning from the activity will be
affected. The teacher who incorporates acknowledgement and
respect for all types of diversity into the classroom ethos will use
the experience and knowledge of the traveller child to add an extra
dimension to the learning programme and to thus make it an un-
forgettable area of knowledge for both traveller and non-traveller
alike. Children will be helped to value each other's cultures whether
that means respecting the fundamental differences in communities or the variations found in family life and everyday lifestyles.

How will this affect the relationship with other traveller children?
In order to plan for learning, the teacher must make an assessment
of the child's abilities and knowledge. However, it would be inappropriate to make assumptions about this child's knowledge of
the remainder of the science curriculum. Most importantly, she
cannot make assumptions about other traveller children's similar
knowledge and experiences. Knowledge of one individual can be
used to inform our understanding of others but generalizations
about communities can be dangerous and misleading.

## Context

It is the responsibility of the school to prepare children for life by
presenting them with a comprehensive curriculum to which all

have equal access. In the first instance, it is imperative to assess all needs and ensure that there is a curriculum match. This is the core of an equal opportunities policy. In practice, this will entail embracing the needs of pupils at all levels of ability and placing differentiated learning materials firmly in position. Those who manage the curriculum must acknowledge the diversity of previous knowledge and skills. But can the prescriptive nature of the National Curriculum accommodate children like Edward? Teachers must use their knowledge and skills to ensure that such children are allowed to learn at the appropriate level, so giving entitlement to a comprehensive curriculum for the full range of children.

The presence of a traveller child on the school roll should mean that staff make it one of their priorities to increase their awareness of traveller culture and its implications within the school environment. There will be a steep learning curve for people working at the school if this is a new experience. Networking with all bodies of people who can support work with travellers in any way must be established to increase awareness and raise the quality of children's learning (Wood 1997).

## The vital ingredients of effective relationships

### Child

What is the child's experience in Cameo 2 in this seemingly pleasant exchange? A conversation has taken place during which the teacher has been relaxed and friendly towards the child in the break time between the serious business of the academic timetable. But the word 'towards' is the crucial one here for it encapsulates the essential core of this conversation. It would be erroneous to use the word 'with' instead; that would imply a sense of togetherness and open exchange that is, in fact, not really present here. On looking more closely at this conversation, it is evident that the differential between teacher and child is carefully preserved and, although the child will probably feel reasonably happy about the conversation, subconsciously he will absorb the fact that the positions of himself and the teacher have been carefully protected with no-one stepping over the lines of demarcation. The 'distance scale' has been preserved. Although there have

*Playground talk*

been no real openings for him to express feelings, there has been some decision making on the part of the child concerning how much he will reveal. The result is what could be termed a 'safe exchange' with few risks taken and few revelations made.

### Teacher

The teacher has made a conscious effort to talk to the child. However, it is not what could be termed a 'normal' conversation of the kind that might be carried out with a friend or family member. Unconsciously, the teacher has used his power to keep the child in place. Therefore the objective of building bridges between the child and himself has not really been achieved, though he may not be aware of this. Mr Brown has missed the opportunity offered by Darren to discover more of his family background. The type of relationship between the child and the teacher is thus established and will reinforce any similar patterns which have been laid down before and equally such patterns are likely to dictate future interactions. The teacher, although not apparently responding to the information concerning the new father, will in most cases have made a mental note of this and discuss its implications with colleagues and possibly record it where appropriate. This will be received in a positive or negative way depending on attitudes and knowledge of the family already formed. The child's current pattern of behaviour may be linked to this new information regarding his family life.

A partnership can begin to develop when there is acknowledgement of the individuality and status of each person in the conversation. However, the teacher holds the stronger position of the two and in the classroom will initiate the patterns of conversation (Hughes and Westgate 1997). Hall and Hall (1988) suggest that in order to bring about change in a relationship, teachers have the power and the authority to initiate the action to achieve an improvement. In the playground, the accepted teacher role is to monitor behaviour, which can provide an opportunity for children to initiate conversation. This did not happen in this scenario.

We could ask a further question. How might this type of conversation be altered to become more meaningful and so advance their relationship on to a more successful plane? The answer must lie in:

1 Making statements rather than use of closed questions (Brown and Wragg 1993) – to encourage extended conversations.
2 Exchanging information – making the relationship a two-way process.
3 Being a listener.
4 Giving space to the other person to ask questions or express opinions.

In this way, a totally different type of relationship will be developed. The type of conversations taking place will determine the relationships which are built. This theme will be expanded in Chapter 3.

**Context**

The mode of conversation in Cameo 2 is necessarily limited in its depth and in what it achieves. However, it has to be acknowledged that there are constraints present in this situation. The teacher is on playground duty and partly responsible for perhaps as many as 150 or so other children – quite a consideration!

From the positive angle, he has made individual contact with the child and had an exchange of sorts. He has also gleaned some valuable information about a crucial part of the child's environment. He must now decide with whom he should share this and how or where it should be recorded. Whole-school policies regarding the sharing of sensitive information must be formulated, and the adults and children should be aware of the extent of the confidentiality of their communications.

The use of power is a central factor here. All the factors that we have considered in the analysis of this cameo could be examined in the larger context of the school. Relationships of staff with work colleagues and with senior management are of necessity determined or affected by the nature of the conversations which take place. In the yet larger forum of local or national government, the method in which information is exchanged will indicate the type or quality of relationships.

## The learning relationship in the primary school

In order for institutions like schools to function effectively, the human relationships found within it demand attention (Hall and Hall 1988). In primary schools, these are varied and consist of adult-to-adult, adult-to-child and child-to-child relationships. However, the relationship between teacher and children is of paramount importance as these interactions help to generate the working ethos of a school (Ainscow and Muncey 1989; Nias 1989). In the introduction to this chapter, we highlighted the different connections that can be formed between people. We would also add the **learning relationship** to this list The important question is on what basis the learning relationship is established. It may be between two equals or there may be a power differential. At the simple level, one can suggest that the child–teacher relationship is between partners of a differing power level. But this will depend on how one perceives the learning process. The type of relationship established with children will result from beliefs about teaching and learning (Moyles 1992). It must be emphasized that this is not exclusive to the teacher side of the partnership as children's understanding and expectations of teaching and learning are of equal importance.

So, the teaching and learning style adopted in the classroom will set the tone for the nature of the relationships between teacher and children. There are many approaches to relations with children and others.

---

**ACTIVITY 2.1**

**The classroom environment**

We have produced a list in Table 2.1 which covers an autocratic approach on the one side and a democratic one on the other. With which of these would you agree? We are sure that for most teachers there is a balance between the two approaches so you may want to rate your response on a scale of 1–5.

*Table 2.1*  Autocratic versus democratic approach

| 1 | →2→3→4→ | 5 |
|---|---|---|
| Teacher takes the lead | Group cooperation encouraged | |
| Teacher makes the decisions | Children encouraged to partake in decisions | |
| Teacher makes the rules | Children encouraged to develop self-discipline | |
| Teacher tells children what to do/learn | Independence in learning encouraged | |
| Teacher knows/child is empty vessel | Acknowledgement of previous knowledge | |
| Teacher's value system is paramount | Accepts children's background | |
| Uses criticism that is mainly negative | Adopts positive approach to discipline | |
| Teacher expects respect | Teacher must earn children's respect | |
| Teacher expects conformity | Teacher values individuals | |

Using the insight gained from this exercise concerning the environment created in your classroom, you will be able to see a pattern based on your particular stance. Whatever this may be, we must consider how children respond to different teaching and learning styles and the effect of that on the learning relationship.

---

## Issues for the child

Children have understandings of relationships formed through their experience. The relationships observed at home and in their immediate environment will be diverse and probably consist of warm loving relationships as well as more negative ones. The variety of individual experiences needs to be understood so that meaningful relationships can be formed within the context of a primary school. The relationships that children form with adults help them develop a basis for understanding social norms and rules. Kutnick (1988) states that the knowledge of different interactions in the home can be transferred to the school context. But the nature of the school setting can be unlike that found in the home. The ratio of adults to children means that behaviour and communication rules and boundaries will be different. Is there enough similarity for this transfer to occur easily without conflict? Most children appear to adapt quickly to the patterns of institutionalized behaviour. But dilemmas are presented, for example, if a child has been brought up to question everything that an adult says or, at the other end of the spectrum, to automatically obey elders without question – then the school context can cause confusion. Children need help to understand why a form of interaction acceptable at home may be different from that expected at school. It may be that a child's knowledge of relationships may have been formed within an extended family, where there is an emphasis on collectiveness. A child of divorced parents may have been challenged by new family structures or the child of a disabled parent may bring experience of a lifestyle where the adult is dependent on the child. The teacher's response to these possible situations will be discussed later in the chapter.

While every child brings diverse experiences from home, the nature of the teacher–child relationship at school can be just as varied. Although there is team teaching found in many primary schools, the majority of children spend most of one year in a close relationship with one teacher. The following year the teaching style and resultant learning relationship may be very different. Children have to learn to accept the differing codes of behaviour expected by each teacher. Headteachers, who have expressed a concern for children to have experience of relating to many adults, have suggested that the employment of classroom assistants offers just such an opportunity (Moyles and Suschitzky 1997a).

Developmentally, children move from a dependency on the teacher in the early years at school to a dual centredness of teacher and peers (Kutnick 1988). Relationships with other children become more central as the child progresses through the primary school and usually at around Year 3 children begin to respond more to their peers. However, criteria for liking or disliking others develop from an early age and are influenced by home, the media and school. These are constantly changing as the child gains in knowledge and experience. The friendship groups children form are often based on gender, race, socio-economic status or physical ability, which can reflect the status level of groups outside the classroom. The policy of inclusion of children with special educational needs in mainstream schools means that children learn about the lives of children different from themselves. Similarly, children in multi-ethnic schools have the opportunity to share experiences of their home and of their religious and cultural lives. This should be a two-way process. But just by being in a multicultural environment does not automatically mean that positive attitudes will develop. Practical ways to encourage children to offer mutual respect will be given later in this chapter.

### Issues for the teacher

It must be acknowledged that the relationships found in primary schools are diverse. A teacher has to establish and maintain individual relationships with 30 or more children as well as developing a collective relationship with the whole class. Just as the children have to adapt to the expectations of behaviour patterns from different teachers so teachers will adapt to some degree their approach to match the personalities and backgrounds of the whole class and its individual members.

As shown in cameo 1, the way that teachers respond to difference affects the relationships established with children. We offer as a further example the adult response to disabled children. An emotional response of pity can produce a particular pattern of behaviour from the child, whereas a response that acknowledges the disability but emphasizes the child's other attributes will allow more independence and self-respect. A patronizing response to a child from an ethnic community can cause indignation and loss of respect for that teacher. Children closely observe the way that we deal with others and try to make sense of these images to develop their understanding and interpretation of the adult world. For example, our dealings with visitors or our approach to domestic or support staff will provide a model for children to copy. Just consider how often you have overheard your own words being used when the role play area is arranged as a school!

### The two-way nature of the teacher–child relationship

It is impossible to examine certain aspects of relationship in terms of the child isolated from the teacher or vice versa for the two are interrelated. Interactions between children and teachers should certainly be based on trust and respect on both sides. The *Oxford Dictionary* defines 'to respect' as 'to treat or regard with deference, esteem or honour'. A traditional view of the educational process is that children should respect their teachers because of their superior knowledge. However there is confusion here because children living at the end of the twentieth century do not automatically give respect to teachers purely because of their profession. This respect has been eroded by changes in society and its values. Teachers know only too well that respect must be earned by providing a secure and positive environment in which children can achieve. The aim must be for mutual respect so that a successful relationship can flourish. So how can teachers form a respect for children? The most important factor influencing learning is what the learner already knows (Ausubel *et al.* 1978). If teachers can acknowledge the experience and skills children have acquired both inside and outside school, then respect will be held and this will be an ingredient in the formation of a good relationship between adult and child. In Cameo 1, the teacher did not acknowledge the child's prior knowledge with the resultant breakdown in the relationship. Teachers trying to cope with the pressures of school life today may find it difficult to see many positive aspects of children's characters and intellectual development. Finding out what an individual can do rather than concentrating on deficiencies is vitally important, as a lack of accord in others' perception of our abilities with that of our own can cause conflict in the relationship and in the potential for learning. This will be discussed further in Chapter 4.

### Self-esteem

One indicator of the quality of the relationship with children will be the level of self-esteem of the teacher. Burns (1982) suggests that teachers who accept themselves are more likely to accept others and teachers who reject themselves are more likely to reject others. A relaxed and confident teacher will create a relaxed atmosphere for learning. Nias (1989) found that teachers rated receiving affection from children as an important part of their professional well-being. Both children and teachers need to feel confident that the parties in a relationship hold positive regard for each other. We have identified being open and accepting as part of a successful relationship. It is easier to express feelings honestly in the knowledge that your partner will accept this. In Cameo 2, the pattern of discourse between teacher and child did not provide opportunity for an open expression of feelings on either side. There should be real conversations in which both talking and listening take place and the owning of particular emotions by the use of the word 'I' will not be feared. Accepting that each individual has their own value system and a right to express this can be considered as an aspect of teacher professionalism. Another element is having ownership of the decision about when and how to express feelings.

Teachers must demonstrate flexibility in their response to diversity and be willing to draw positive attitudes towards children's differing experiences. The child from an extended family may well be able to take cooperative decisions in group work, easily accepting others views, and may work effectively towards a group or class image. Such a child may not project as an individual as much as others in the class. As teachers we should make use of this knowledge in providing appropriate classroom experiences. A child living in a complex family setting of step-parent and half-siblings may bring sophisticated skills of negotiation, sharing and communication. The child of a disabled parent may be more independent, emotionally and physically, and likewise have sophisticated decision-making and organizational skills This child's experiences may lead to expectations of being heard by adults. In these ways, the children in a school bring a wide range of abilities and knowledge to the classroom scene.

We can learn much from examining in detail the way in which we interact with different children in the classroom. Work carried out by Morgan and Dunn (1988) offers an example of how research can provide insight into classroom relationships. They studied early years' classes to observe the way children interact with each other and with their teachers and whether gender had any bearing on the levels of obtrusiveness. They found that different teacher reactions to 'visible children' are based mainly on feelings that these children may constitute a potential disturbance. 'Invisible children', however, present different problems for the teacher. Such children may be shy but content, or anxious and withdrawn. Large numbers of children can prevent the busy teacher from giving a fair share of attention to all, with the visible, often male, child demanding unfair amounts of time. Morgan and Dunn suggest that assertive children learn quickly that this behaviour pattern brings rewards in both attention and status. Assertiveness is not only associated with gender but can have a basis in cultural or social status awareness.

## Issues for the school

A school community is made up of people of differing ages, roles and backgrounds. During a day, a child will be in contact with children of the same age, those a few years older or younger, teachers, support staff, other children's families and a variety of visitors to the school. In Chapter 1 we defined the identity of a school and how the power differentials operate. The ethos that has evolved for the individual school will influence the nature of the relationships within it. Part of the hidden curriculum of a school is the type and variety of relationships found there. Children learn from observing the structures in the school, which then give messages about relationships.

You might like to consider the structures found in your school or others that you know (Activity 2.2).

### Grouping

The opportunities for children to establish child–child relationships are governed by the school context. Thomas (1985) suggests that a school's method of grouping children can form part of the hidden curriculum. For example, how much interaction there is with children of different ages, and whether the children work in pairs or collaborative groups for part of the day, is essentially controlled within the framework of the classroom management and has important effects. Classroom organization often means that children sit in ability groups for part of the day. Pollard (1985) found that during a school year children moved towards

---

**ACTIVITY 2.2**

**Hidden messages**

Try to answer the following questions. Do they reveal any hidden messages in the school?

1 Do you allow the children to call the only male member of staff 'sir' and the others 'Miss'?
2 Are the only ethnic-minority members of staff the ancillaries or bilingual support teachers?
3 What facilities are there for disabled parents and visitors?

The implications of the answers to these questions are far reaching and should provide you with a deeper insight into the ethos of the school.

---

friendship groupings based on academic ability. This was due to working together but also the feedback used by teachers which reinforced notions of ability.

Gender attitudes in the school may determine whether single-gender groupings are formed in the playground. For example, if girls are encouraged to play football then more mixed gender friendship groups may develop. Also, strong antiracist practices given prominence in a school may encourage more mixed race friendships between children. If there is an emphasis on sport, musical achievement or academic success and if competition to win is given prominence over the importance of taking part, then account must be taken of how underachievers in these fields will be handled. While it is vital to promote excellence, it can be questioned whether the gap widens between achievers and non-achievers as the latter's self-esteem is lowered.

Whole-school approaches to handling negative attitudes by one child against another must be considered. Gaine (1995) states that teachers who have not considered their own assumptions and attitudes towards race find difficulty accepting that negative attitudes are present amongst the children. Teachers who work with students from ethnic communities for the first time may never consider the possibility of a child making a racist remark to a black teacher. Time needs to be allocated for whole staff discussion to formulate a policy which all feel comfortable in implementing.

**STRATEGIES**

**Observing children's relationship formation**

Here is one suggestion of how a teacher might seek to explore ways in which children handle their relationships.

The children are formed into a group in order to organize the writing of a newspaper. They are to discuss and suggest ways in which the work could be done. Furthermore, they are to decide upon the particular tasks which each individual might perform. It is important to understand that the children are to be left alone in order to deal with this task. A challenge has been created for them of how they will create a suitable working environment to achieve their aim. We have a situation requiring some collaborative group work and some decision making. The usefulness in this situation for the teacher will not be to focus on the finished result, although no doubt that will be valuable, but on the insights that will be gained into the processes of the children's learning. In order to gain these insights, observation must take place. There are several ways in which this may be achieved:

- Sit nearby, without being intrusive, and watch and listen to the procedures which will take place. A notepad will obviously be useful as it will be impossible to recall everything at a later date.
- Alternatively, leave a tape recorder with the group to record what is being said and listen to it later. It will be most effective if the children are accustomed to this happening so that they behave naturally and virtually ignore its presence. Of course, this will not identify any significant body language. But, listening only to the conversation will probably allow you to concentrate on the implications.
- Ask a colleague, as an objective person, to undertake the observation also and share the findings later. By doing this, you will eliminate a subjective interpretation that may occur due to your closeness to the children.

But the question may well be asked, how can this observation be of any importance? Observations are commonly understood within the early years' classroom and are sometimes considered to be routine but of limited significance. We must make sure that we know what the observations are likely to reveal. This should highlight a whole range of behaviour and stances based upon the individual child's experiences, behaviour patterns, personality and interpersonal skills already acquired – the list is endless!

In order for the observation to be valuable, it is necessary for the teacher to decide on some of the focal points in advance. This is probably not as easy as it sounds and it would undoubtedly be useful to discuss with colleagues first and to work in some form of partnership. But some pointers here might prove useful.

- Are there children who appear to take a leading role in speech or behaviour. Do others listen to them and do what they suggest?
- Is there another child who challenges that leadership role? For how long?
- Are there children willing to acquiesce to the suggestions of others?
- What of the quiet children in the group? Are they gentle but assertive? Do they listen to others? Are they passive or active through their quietness?
- How do the noisier children really behave? Are they merely the 'clowns'; are they aggressive or are they really leaders?
- Gender issues – boys and girls behave in certain ways as a result of a variety of influences. Are these from cultural backgrounds, religious dictates or family structures?
- Role play – children both act out the roles with which they are familiar and probably comfortable, and also use opportunities to test out other roles which they have observed. Are they ready to be encouraged to move away from tried-and-tested roles to those which are new and would open up new avenues?
- Interaction skills – some children will be starting to learn negotiating techniques and others will seem to have no knowledge of such things. Will some children be able to work in cooperation with others while other children will be strongly individualistic?

You could amend this list as appropriate to your setting.

The main factor which must be considered is that the observation needs to be as definitive and detailed as possible. Its value will be in direct relation to the depth which is attained. When you examine your findings, there may well be some surprises! Again, share it with a colleague. Analyse and reflect! Test out your findings. Was your discovery a 'one off' or is it part of a regular pattern of children's approaches? The potential outcome could be:

- A greater understanding of those children, for example who are leaders, followers, and where there are gender or cultural influences – but also some more unanswered questions. You will be able to move on to more such observing as a way to answer some of your queries.

- A greater ability to meet the needs of individual children for building up a greater knowledge will also help to create a deeper understanding of them. You have thus begun to create a continuous profile, and therefore a relationship between teacher and child based on knowledge and a deeper understanding of individual characteristics.

In such activities, the more you do it the better you become!

---

**ACTIVITY 2.3**

**Children in pairs**

This activity examines the way in which two individual children rather than a group of children communicate with each other and therefore develop a particular kind of relationship. You will find differences between behaviour patterns found in group and those in pair work.

**The task**

Two children are to either use a piece of equipment or to organize something together. This can be any common classroom activity. Remember, it is the everyday which will often give us the key to understanding.

**The partners**

This can be made up in a variety of ways depending upon the area to be explored by the teacher.

- two children who are already friends;
- a child experiencing difficulties with one not experiencing difficulties;
- an older child with a younger one;
- an established member of the class with a new arrival;
- a fluent English speaker with a child who is still establishing himself at Level 1 in that particular language.

A few guidelines to act as starting points for observation.

1 What kind of body language is used and how often? Is it friendly, aggressive, appropriate?

2 Are they able to negotiate?
3 Does one child feel the need to dominate?
4 Do either of the children show a need to adopt an adult role?
5 Do either of the children show an ability to help the other?
6 Are literacy/numeracy skills used more by one child?
7 Are they able to work well as a partnership?
8 Do they need to seek the aid of an adult?

Observation should again be recorded and then shared with colleagues. It will give some indication of the strengths and abilities of each child and also the ways in which she or he may benefit from future guidance and opportunities. Remember also that the class will be able to make wise use of the strengths shown. For example, a child sympathetic to the needs of others should be able sometimes to lead other children to recognize such needs; a child able to lead firmly and fairly will be able to use such skills again; a child working well in a partnership will probably be able to do so again in similar circumstances.

There will undoubtedly be many other discoveries which you will make. Behaviour and language will often reveal the same characteristics. In these early years, of course, for some children one or the other will tend to dominate although it can also be surprising how soon a balance is established between the two. Children may have a preference for a group of children such as those of the same sex or same race but this does not imply a negative attitude towards others in general. But group or collaborative work can be used to develop positive attitudes.

**ACTIVITY 2.4**

**Teacher–child relationships in the classroom**

Now try this activity to help you to analyse your relationships in the classroom and evaluate them effectively. How do you respond to the following?

1 The child who is habitually late.
2 The child who frequently cries in class.
3 The child who constantly needs a friend with whom to do everything.
4 The child who is always the first with their hand up.

If you are irritated by the crying child, is it because you are a confident person who rarely cries especially in public or do you have knowledge of the child's background, which has influenced your response? Do you empathize with the child's family situation? From where does your view come?

1 Your background.
2 Your value system.
3 Your knowledge of the child's family situation.
4 Outside pressures, such as too many children in the class and constraints of the National Curriculum.

We can use the knowledge gained from the analysis of our relationships with individual children in our class to help us move forward towards the development of a positive and constructive view of each child.

## Conclusion

As teachers, we need to develop greater awareness of the import-ance of relationships with children and give a high priority to developing interpersonal skills. This can only be achieved if we regard communication as the most effective way to establish suc-cessful relationships. The development of relationships can be a way to build bridges but they are of little use if no one is able to cross over to the other side. Communication from one side to the other must take place if the bridge is to be of any value. In our cameo in the Introduction to this book (page 1), the staff needed to build bridges, using good relationships and effective commun-ication, to ensure success with their project. Chapter 3 examines communication, which is complex and dependent on a wide vari-ety of factors. In order to appreciate and utilize such complexity, we will seek to indicate ways in which we can analyse and use different approaches to communication.

# 3

# Communication: it's good to talk!

**Cameo 1**

It is soon to be parents' evening at Witchell Primary School and Mr Owen, teacher of a Year 4 class, is reading the replies from parents regarding their appointments. Dean's mother, Mrs Jackson, has requested, as she is deaf, that Dean should accompany her to the interview and use sign language for the translation of the conversation.

**Cameo 2**

Karen, a child in Mrs Green's class, regularly interrupts her with questions and comments many of which are not particularly relevant to the occasion. Sometimes these remarks, accompanied by some facial expressions, produce a kind of 'clowning' effect which can be highly amusing to the rest of the class.

**Cameo 3**

The children in a Year 1 classroom are reaching the end of a busy morning during which a wide range of materials have been used. The classroom is strewn with books, papers, pens and pencils together with a collection of items such as glue, scissors, gummed papers. Suddenly realizing the time, the teacher, Mr McDonald, quickly says: 'Tidy up and then line up for dinner.' The speed with which different children respond to this instruction and the effectiveness of their tidying up varies enormously.

## Introduction

One way that children interpret the learning context is by trying to understand the modes of communication found there. As shown in Chapter 2, the establishment of positive relationships is a vital part of effective primary education. The use of language in relationship formation requires examination and, in particular, in terms of culturally diverse relationships. Language is a total system, a structure of interrelated elements and relationships (Whitehead 1996b). We acknowledge this and, within the scope of this chapter, place a parameter by focusing specifically on the oracy aspect of communication. By this we mean talk, both verbal and non-verbal, and listening. In fact, as Hall and Hall (1988: 57) suggest, 'the impact of non-verbal communication is potentially much greater than that of verbal'.

Language cannot be considered outside of its context. One person can generate utterances and gestures which are meaningful statements to another person only if both parties share knowledge of that communication system. Communicators therefore require a shared contextual framework to achieve understanding. In cross-cultural settings this may not be easy to establish. For example, responses would be unpredictable to the other party if discussing an event of which only one partner has experience. However, true understanding requires more even than a shared context as two people can witness the same event but interpret it in many different ways dependent on their *communication background*.

What aspects of language are 'put in the cupboard' and only used after school is over for the day? Most children have experience of the more established forms of English usage from their early years. When they become members of the primary school community, they will have to communicate with the other members of this environment and the established form of communication may be different in some way to the child's first language. So we should ask how acceptable other language forms are in school and whether the child needs to abandon its first language all together or put it in the cupboard, only retrieving it at home time. If first language is not respected, then the messages that children receive show that their home life and the people they love and respect are not valued. If teachers have to hide away their first language or regional accent and only communicate in the established form, then they also receive messages that under-value their backgrounds.

Because of the diversity in communication and in order to achieve receptivity from each partner, there needs to be a recognition of both the stable and variable factors in language contexts. In this chapter, we will consider those factors that are constant in all forms of communication and those that are particular to one context. A second theme will be to examine the power of language as used by teacher or child within a learning relationship.

## Recognition of special skills of communication

### Child

For Dean, in Cameo 1 many aspects of the situation are familiar. In the home environment he is accustomed to using and inter-preting sign language as a normal means of effective commun-ication. Similarly, he regularly transfers appropriately from the use of sign language to the spoken word and is therefore a bilin-gual child using both means of communication in his everyday life. The particular challenge here will be to take the role of inter-preter between the two adults. He needs to be able to under-stand and relay both the words and ideas so that a rapport can effectively be achieved. Moreover, the fact that he is the subject of the conversation presents a possible dilemma for him and for Mr Owen.

### Teacher

For most people, the type of situation in Cameo 1 will present something of a challenge. It is likely that Mr Owen will have relied on oracy in meetings with hearing parents and so the need to use the skills of an interpreter presents a new factor. However, we hasten to underline that in this cosmopolitan society there are many schools who use interpreters for parents' evenings where a variety of languages are the norm within a community. This particular instance does, however, contain a somewhat different dimension. Mr Owen need not feel undermined in any way but approach it professionally and confidently. When should he look at Dean and when at Mrs Jackson? It will be important to give close attention to both the child and the parent so that any one of the three does not feel isolated or undervalued. An important factor will be whether sensitive issues concerning Dean can be discussed when he is translating. This, of course, raises the issue of parent and teacher discussing children when they are not present. If children are to take responsibility for their own learning then perhaps they should attend such discussions. Acknowledgement should be given to the additional ability displayed by this child and encouragement given to build on these communication skills. It also presents an opportunity within the wider curriculum to introduce the whole class to life in a home with a deaf family member.

## Context

Where schools are familiar with the use of many languages among their pupils and have the correct quota of bilingual staff to support this situation, the event only presents a further step in an already well-established pattern of language behaviour. The school has a responsibility to establish policy concerning the provision made for diversity in every form. It is essential that policy statements acknowledge and promote linguistic diversity. In order to assist in the implementation of policy, schools should consider the means of providing advice for teachers on how to respond to the situation in which one person is speaking on behalf of another.

## The use of language in the relationships found within the primary classroom

### Child

Karen, in Cameo 2, is demanding attention and is unwilling to be an 'anonymous' member of the group. Therefore there is a challenge to Mrs Green's position. This is particularly true where 'clowning' occurs and the child is 'playing to the gallery'. It is a bid for power by using certain patterns of language and the child will have copied such uses from home experiences. But we must not make the error of assuming that this is necessarily malicious. It may, in fact, be a result of a basic insecurity although it may equally be a result of a determination to be at the forefront. It could well be an indication of a child unsure of their personal identity. If so, the communication is in fact rather like the layers of an onion and has to be gradually peeled away to reach the core of meaning.

### Teacher

The teacher's position as leader is definitely being challenged. The flow of speech is interrupted and the attention of the group is lost. A range of strategies has to be used to maintain the teacher's position as group leader and to deal with the individual at the same time. In Cameo 2, knowledge of Karen's background will help the teacher to make judgements concerning whether to ignore the behaviour or insist on conformity. Giving praise and attention for positive behaviour and taking time outside the lesson to give Karen opportunity to talk will alleviate the situation to some extent. Her energy can be directed into areas in which she demonstrates ability so that she and Mrs Green can feel a level of success.

### Context

As Cameo 2 shows, the use of language can be a powerful tool. Classroom teachers use forms of language that children must learn to decode and children learn to use language to achieve attention from the teacher. The use of professional jargon can be used as a tool of power by school senior management, local education authority officials and government bodies. If the requirements of official documents are to be carried out then the language used must be accessible to the teacher in the classroom, who is implementing the actions. Parents should also have access to information concerning all aspects of primary education and the means should be provided to ensure that language barriers are removed to allow this to occur.

### Finding a shared understanding of language

### Child

The most obvious factor affecting the children in Cameo 3 is that they must be able to understand exactly what Mr McDonald's instructions imply so that they can respond to them correctly. 'Tidy up' as an instruction at home will have meant something rather different and 'line up' will not have been part of the home language but will rather be part of a whole new range of communication obtained from the school environment. If the children are to respond effectively to instructions of this kind given by the teacher over and above the working buzz of the classroom, the pupils also have to be able to acquire the skill of listening on two levels. They must be able to communicate with their fellow pupils for work purposes but also always to have an awareness of his voice giving general instructions to the class as a whole. The children's response to instructions will vary depending upon:

- Their absorption in their task.
- Their ability to actually 'hear' and process instructions.
- Their previous experience of decoding instructions.
- Their willingness to respond appropriately.

Therefore, the degree of response will vary according to the individual child. It follows that the actual depth of communication will be influenced by all of these factors.

## Teacher

In Cameo 3, Mr McDonald is obviously making some assumptions here, that the children will know exactly what is meant and that the pupils will respond to the commands quickly and efficiently (Moyles 1992). Therefore, this situation is really a result of previous periods of training during which procedures in the classroom will have been explained to the children. The children will therefore have learnt what the two instructions 'to tidy up' and 'to line up' really imply. It is a learnt code of communication with specific implications. It is, in fact, the communication of an institution rather than a friendship conversation. The children's communication background will determine how quickly they have learnt this code. Moreover, individual teachers will also have different expectations of the outcomes of this request, which will be determined by the teacher's value system. An expectation of 'tidy' may be very varied in terms of the children's independence or perhaps who does the majority of the work – girls or boys!

In life outside school, we ask questions mainly when we need to find an answer to something that we do not know. In school, we as teachers ask questions about subjects to which we know the answer but the purpose of the questioning is very different. Why do we ask so many questions? Children quickly learn to guess what is in the teacher's mind and answer accordingly. The Leverhulme Primary Project (Wragg 1991) found that the reasons given by teachers for use of questions were mainly to encourage thought and understanding, checking children's understanding and knowledge and to gain attention to the task.

## Context

There are many different language codes found within society and most of these are present in primary schools. During the school day, there will be playground talk, staffroom talk, the language of instruction, informative talk in text books, narrative in story books, and information giving and receiving. Adults switch between codes and children also learn to adapt. But, as with any other subject, the learning curve is gradual and the actual speed of it will vary. For young people in a school environment, there are many such learning curves all taking place at the same time. It is remarkable how well they achieve in such a demanding situation. In particular the need to progress well in the field of communication is crucial. The more successful they become the more their progress in all other spheres will be influenced.

### Communication issues for the child

*First language* is the language that is predominant in a child's home and is the one that the child first learns to use. This may not be the language of the wider society. It includes regional accents and dialects with distinctive words and idioms, ethnic community languages and modes of communication such as British Sign Language. Other variables may include the frequent use of expletives and other ranges of vocabulary and sentence length. First language is an aspect of our identity and one of the valuable items to be stored securely (see Introduction to this chapter and Chapter 1). Whitehead (1996a) states that an attack on our first language can be insulting and alienating. It does not need to be an open attack but innuendo and non-recognition of a child's home mode of communication can cause harm to self-esteem. Pollard (1996) concludes that linguistic factors reinforce children's emerging identities if these are consistent with the expectations of the school but where inconsistency is found, this can lead to insecurity.

It must be acknowledged that for many children there is more than one language present in the daily communication of the home – one example being that used by family members and the presence of television and radio perhaps presenting a different form. By this we do not mean that the received pronunciation of the BBC is always different from the language of the home but the use of slang, or 'gutter English' as the Secretary of State for Education in 1997 named this form common in TV programmes, may present a different usage from that found in other households. How can children sort out the many patterns and codes of *acceptable* language? To whom and in what circumstances is it *acceptable*?

It is not only the use of the actual spoken word or the grammatical structure that is important but our response to language, the meanings we interpret and the resultant actions. Children must certainly know how to communicate in Standard English to survive in British society. Acceptance of this is an important ingredient in any school's language policy. It should not be interpreted as a degradation or dissolution of the child's first language but a recognition of bi- or multilingualism as an asset. Children need to learn which language is appropriate to use in which context and need encouragement to be skilled and effective communicators in any of their languages. The power of the language is found in its use and interpretation.

## Communication issues for the teacher

As teachers, we need to consider the aspects of communication as suggested by the National Oracy Project (Norman 1990), which are social, communicative and cognitive. These three aspects of talk result in collaborative learning.

### Social aspect

People are naturally gregarious and need to socialize. Within the school context, socialization means children with each other, adult with adult and child to adult and takes place both on an individual and group level. Talk is a necessary (but not exclusive) ingredient in socialization and functions as the vehicle for sharing pleasure and enjoyment, offering and accepting support in times of difficulties, sharing experiences and expressing feelings. A child's main purpose for communication at home is primarily socializing and survival. As the number of relationships formed gradually expand from those of the immediate family and neighbourhood to a wider group of community members, so the range of language skills also expands. Teachers need to recognize that children can 'gain access to the shared consciousness of their culture by the concepts, metaphors and frames of reference found in language' (Smith and Cowie 1991: 281).

## Informative aspect of talk

Language structures our lives and provides the means of receiving and using information. The often used statement 'knowledge is power' is dependent on the successful use of communication skills to use the 'knowledge' effectively. The use of language can also reflect the hierarchy in the classroom where it is not always the teacher who is in control. Children can use communication as power over the teacher by constantly interrupting to gain attention or telling longer and longer anecdotes so as not to do maths. Children may have differing levels of communication power depending on their skills at using the classroom language.

## Learning aspect of talk

The significance of language in learning has been widely documented (Donaldson 1978; Wells 1987). Vygotsky (see Wood 1988: 24) argued that language structures the thinking process and through interaction the child progresses. It is through social interaction with other people that children negotiate meaning. They need to listen to and learn from others in order to achieve collaborative learning. So cognitive development depends on the use of language (Smith and Cowie 1991). But young children have to learn to decode the type of language used in schools and understand why it is different from language patterns used at home.

## Communication issues for the school

In British society the culture language is English, which is the dominant language of commerce, the media, leisure activities and of course, education. Pattanayak (1981) states: 'when one language is confined to the intimate domain and another language is used in all other domains, the latter may be called the *'culture language'* (our emphasis). Many children in British schools possess an ability to speak in the culture language and that of the 'intimate domain' but not always with equal competence. Thus a definition of bilingual is difficult as the term can apply to those who possess at least one of the language skills (listening, speaking, reading or writing) to a minimal degree in their second language or to those who have an equal balance of fluency in two languages. Whitehead (1998) uses the term 'successive bilingual' referring to children starting school with a resultant imbalance between the first and second language.

How the educational establishment responds to bilingual children from ethnic communities was reported by Swann (1985: 399) and specific strategies are now in place in schools with a high multi-ethnic population. Swann's first model ('Bilingual Education: the structuring of the school's work to allow for the use of a pupil's mother tongue as a medium of instruction alongside English') is found in early years classrooms where the children have a limited knowledge of English. The child's first language is the channel through which his or her learning is developed. However, once the child is competent in English then first language support is often withdrawn as *the problem is solved*. Swann's second model ('Mother Tongue Maintenance: the development of a pupil's fluency in his or her mother tongue as an integral part of the curriculum') enhances the bilingual child's sense of self-esteem and identity also ensuring that she or he is not linguistically cut off from family and community. It is the value placed on the bilingualism that is crucial. In our society, the same status is not accorded to being bilingual in English and Urdu as to that given to an ability to speak English and French. Although Swann was reporting on ethnic minorities, the principles are the same for other forms of communication, for example British Sign Language users.

Social conventions and cultural norms are learnt through the medium of language and it is through this that traditions are maintained. Conversely, this heartfelt statement (source unknown) was spoken by an elder of the Inuit community in Canada: 'If you want to kill a culture then educate its children in another language.' This situation is faced not only by aboriginal people around the world but also by immigrant groups. The medium of instruction may be that of the majority language but the use of the child's first language must also be acceptable within the school context. It is easier to make provision for teaching of first language when a substantial proportion of the school population speak the same language but provision for a few children has to be considered in the light of practicalities and cost effectiveness. However, as is implicit in the Inuit leader's comments, it is the valuing of the language that encourages the children to maintain their cultural background.

A high priority is given by most early years teachers, and other primary teachers, to language development as a key to all-round development. However, this emphasis often means that the child can be overly judged by their competence in language. This can result in negative assessments, which do not reflect conceptual competence or social and creative ability but become solely based on language capabilities. Children from families where English is a second language are still on occasion described as having *no language*, ignoring their capability in other forms of communication.

It must be acknowledged that an overwhelming need of all families in Britain is for their children to succeed within the requirements of British society. This means mastering the English language and using it in appropriate contexts. The added ingredient of a second language makes for complex work when coupled with a hearing impairment. For example, which language should children use for signing? If they only learn British Sign Language then can they communicate with parents whose knowledge of English may be limited? Another dilemma found in work with young bilinguals is the language levels found in the home. Young parents who have grown up in a second-generation lingualism may not always have the language skills to support their children's learning. The negative attitudes that were apparent in the 1970s towards first-language use in school means that many can only function at a low level and for similar reasons their English needs were not fully met. This can hamper the language development of their own children today. If first language is well developed then children can apply the acquired skills to the second language (Siraj-Blatchford 1994).

**STRATEGIES**

**A language line**

In earlier chapters, we have suggested that the knowledge
of an individual's identity is crucial in order to develop
relationships. One aspect of identity is language and in the
following activity we invite you to trace your life's language
line. It is fun to do and can be used in a variety of contexts
and for various purposes. We leave it to your imagination to
make the most of it!

**ACTIVITY 3.1**

**Individuality and identity**

Draw a simple line diagram which traces your individual life
story through various aspects of language. These aspects play
a major role in your development and serve to present a picture
of your individuality and identity. The following (see Figure 3.1)
is an example from one of the authors.

There will inevitably be areas of influence which have been
inadvertently omitted from Figure 3.1. We will now point out
a few small areas in this particular language line where certain
influences are reflected to help you to perceive the moulding
influence that language alone can have upon us.

- 'As a child growing up in Wales and Shropshire, a common
  expression of disgust in the home was "Ach y fi!" It was only
  much later in life that I realized that this was, in fact, a Welsh
  expression.'
- 'A memory of my grandfather holding up a sock and saying,
  "Where's the marra to this one?" Although Shropshire born
  and bred he had married a lass from the North East of
  England where the word "marra" denotes a "pal/buddy/other
  one of the pair".'
- 'During teacher training most of our fellow students spoke
  with strong Yorkshire or Lancashire accents so that my own
  lilting Shropshire was markedly different. The inevitable
  teasing took place to the extent that I became determined
  to lose my accent as soon as possible. Then I would not
  stand out in the crowd as an oddity.'

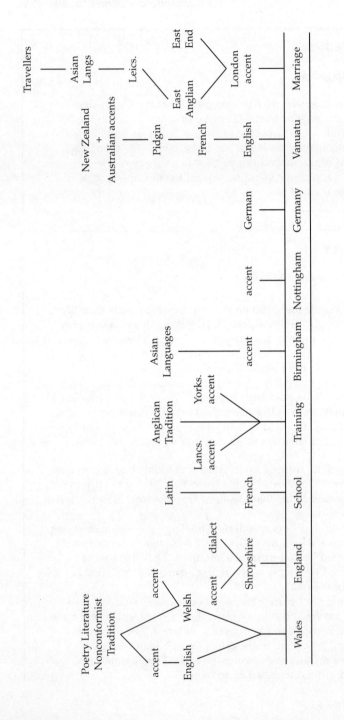

**Language Line**

*Figure 3.1*

Upon investigating your own language line you will soon discover an amazing carnival of influences which have made you who you are. They will be part of the reason why you behave in certain ways whether it be by acceptance of what they represent or rejection. It is part of what is sometimes called our personal 'baggage'. We carry it around with us wherever we may be. It forms part of our identity.

The next stage, after discovering these influences upon ourselves is to recognize that there is an equally diverse and interesting language line for every individual. It can tell us something about them. We can apply the process whenever we have information about individual pupils. But remember, this is one aspect only of a complex person. Every other aspect you may choose to study will reveal a similar kaleidoscope of facets: for example, eating habits, celebrations and holiday patterns.

Repeat this exercise, as far as you are able, for a child in your class. It will obviously be most effective where you know some details about the child's home environment. Drawing upon your own remembered experiences, try to estimate how many adjustments the child has had to make. Assess to what extent he or she has been successful in this adjusting. Consider this alongside all the other new things which are to be learnt in both the social and academic fields and consider just how demanding it is. No wonder some children succeed but others appear to need a period of time in which to find themselves and operate efficiently.

## Relationships as a ladder of progression

As relationships develop over time and changes occur in feelings and behaviour, so the use of language during the progress of the relationship changes. We would suggest the ladder of progression (Figure 3.2) of a relationship as seen through the use of language. If analysed, a natural friendship relationship will probably gradually progress from formal and brief exchanges to those much lengthier and less formal. What begins as the exchange of the necessary language for the business of the day will gradually change to reflect a wish to exchange information and views. A further development will be the sharing of feelings on a more personal level. Friendly banter and teasing may well become a natural part of the relationship: the type of language will develop in parallel with the relationship and the range of vocabulary will also be affected.

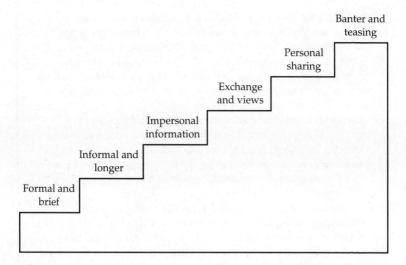

*Figure 3.2*

We raise the question of whether this ladder of language use is common to all cultures. It may be that the rungs are in a different order or the speed of progress up the ladder may vary. Also, do the same gender relationships progress in the same way and do the circumstances of cross-cultural relationships affect the movement up the ladder?

---

**ACTIVITY 3.2**

**Child-to-child relationship**

The above is an adult-to-adult relationship, but how would a child-to-child relationship and pattern of language look? Using your knowledge of the children with whom you work, create a similar ladder for them. Make an observation of two or more children working collaboratively. Assess to what extent the relationships reflect the suggested ladder. You may have also included in-group vocabulary, secret words and body language. If there are differences then try to seek an explanation and readjust the ladder accordingly. The activity will be all the more valuable if it is in conjunction with a colleague so that you are able to discuss and analyse the findings.

What does this mean in the primary classroom? The result of this activity gives us knowledge of children's level of relationships and therefore what our expectations can be realistically at each stage on the ladder. For example, we may be able to pinpoint why a child is isolated from the group or define the factors of a particular group identity. This knowledge will inform our actions, for example, in the case of an isolated child who can then be encouraged to gain access to the group and children made sensitive to the needs of others outside their group. Children should be taught to be open about group languages, codes and resultant behaviour patterns, and share their language with others. We would underline the need for balance between the recognition and celebration of diversity in language with being alert to the needs of minority individual or group members.

Likewise, in the teacher–child relationship of the school, oral communication will reflect the type and depth of the relationship. Trust between the individuals concerned will enhance the quality of language used so that it progresses beyond the basic level to a more adventurous and sophisticated one. In such circumstances the child's language will have a greater opportunity to develop. Pollard (1996) suggests that the style and uses of language are very powerful indicators of the ethos of a school and the type of relationships found there. You could try a language ladder for the adult-to-adult relationships in your school. What does it tell you about the ethos and the messages being given to children?

## Conclusion

The important question that needs to be asked is who influences children's language or mode of communication? Brice Heath (1983) describes the different ways of using language as found in two different communities. These differences were dependent on the family structures and the resultant experiences available to the children, for example, learning by heart or narrating stories with a moral. She concludes that neither community's ways prepared the children for the school's ways. So children come together from different experiences of language and are taught by someone with yet a different experience of language within a context with different expectations. Surprising that they learn anything at all! We all have to consider where the languages spoken in each individual school fit into the diverse pattern of language use in Britain today.

Communication in the primary classroom has many different purposes and therefore different structures. We have analysed some distinct areas but teachers should realize that all areas have equal importance and are used by both children and adults. We need an acute awareness of them and require highly developed skills to use them effectively. These include listening skills, the ability to choose correct forms of language to match appropriateness of situations, awareness of different uses of language and being able to make errors without feeling constrained.

In writing about communication, we have made reference to the many modes employed for a wide variety of purposes. There are direct links with these forms of communication and their effectiveness in creating meaningful relationships in the classroom. In Chapter 4 we will discuss how these are influential in establishing a suitable climate for learning. As the teachers in the introductory Cameo (page 1) discussed ways to construct a strong storage cupboard for their valuable items, so our next chapter will examine the elements that we feel form the structure of an effective learning environment for primary children.

# 4

# A climate for learning: what will the cupboard be made of?

**Cameo 1**

Sharon Sims, who originates from a working-class background, drives to school in a ten-year-old 2CV. The children in her class of 9-year-olds are mainly from executive type housing and go horse-riding and ice-skating at the weekends. During the Christmas holiday, several children have been to Florida while Sharon has spent her holiday buying essentials in the sales and working on a policy document.

**Cameo 2**

Wayne, a boy in a class of Key Stage 2 children is constantly presenting staff and peer group with challenges brought about by his behaviour patterns, which are strikingly different from those around him. As he is underachieving academically, the teacher, Mrs Patel, is exasperated and regularly feels that she is able to predict what will happen during the day. In fact, this seems to be amazingly true as the boy spends more and more time outside the headteacher's door.

## Introduction

Having considered factors that are part of the establishment of a climate for learning, such as assumptions about relationships and modes of communication, the next step is to examine actual teaching and learning, together with the factors that we consider as having an important influence on these. Formerly in the English primary education system, individual teachers had considerable control over the creation of their own classroom environment and as a result the teaching and learning in each classroom was very varied but potentially lacked cohesion. Since the Education Reform Act and the instigation of Ofsted inspections, there is more conformity in curriculum and methodology, at least due in part to certain perceptions held in schools about Ofsted requirements. However, it is still the individual teacher's responsibility to create the climate for learning in the class. So on what basis are the choices concerning the classroom environment made? Pedagogy is based on personal values and principles which are formed by an individual's experiences and cultural background (Clark and Peterson 1986; Day 1993). We will now examine the factors influencing the teacher's teaching style, the children's learning style and the school's ethos. As with most issues in primary education, the creation of a climate for learning is extremely complex and incorporates a combination of several contributory factors.

### Children's views of teachers and teachers' views of children

The immediate questions raised by cameo 1 are how does Sharon Sims feel about the children in her care and does this have any effect on her teaching? She may decide not to ask the children to share their experiences over the holiday and rarely refer to their home life. This sends certain messages to the class and influences the attitude it has towards the teacher.

### Child

The background of these 9-year-olds may have provided knowledge of the way that professionals, such as teachers, live and they will have heard talk at home which enables them to challenge the teacher's authority. Their knowledge and first-hand experiences may seem at times superior to that of the teacher and can constitute a perceived threat. Also, to such children wealth may be valued as a mark of status and the teacher's lack of obvious wealth may affect their level of respect. So a mismatch of value systems between child and teacher can result in obstacles to establishing a shared learning environment. This will equally be true in any situation where social background is reversed.

## Teacher

Sharon Sims must recognize the value of the children's extensive experiences and make use of what they bring. In all areas, teachers must utilize the ideas, emotions, relationships and extended knowledge arising from the socio-economic situation in which children live. Where there are differences between the children's and the teacher's backgrounds, whether it is the situation in Cameo 1 or the more usual scenario of middle-class teachers working in schools in deprived areas, the same principles apply.

Teachers must explore children's experiences and knowledge whatever they are and become attuned to their personal/professional feelings about these. Sharon Sims needs to recognize that, as a result of her value system, she is inclined to scorn the children's materialism and this can affect her dealings with the class, and may override the potential for extending the children's experiences. She needs to be a facilitator, who helps children learn to value and interpret experiences in the light of extending knowledge and ability to cross-reference with previous information. It is important that the teacher presents her experiences to the children and helps them to evaluate these also so enabling them to view diversity positively.

## Context

The materials and resources provided in the school should reflect the children's background and experiences and extend them. The school's statement of aims should be clear about recognizing the differences in children's home lives and using the development plan to ensure that resources are appropriately provided. It is important to examine commonalities in children's experiences and build on these to develop the curriculum.

### Looking for the positives

### Child

In Cameo 2 the boy is showing himself to be a disruptive influence and is an underachiever academically. For some reason beyond his own understanding, he experiences difficulties in his work which he is unable to explain to anyone and these difficulties are obviously not changed by any support or tuition he is currently achieving. He knows within himself that he is not stupid or lacking in ability and yet, in some strange way, he is not producing work which reflects his intelligence. Members of his peer group signify their recognition of his lack of success with the usual labels. The child feels angry, frustrated and, eventually, determined to 'show them'. The result is a catalogue of unfortunate events during which he reveals himself as a nuisance apparently unwilling to cooperate.

Unfortunately, the cycle of underachievement is now firmly in place and it will be a big undertaking to break it: the pupil has a label which spells out 'unsatisfactory' and 'a nuisance'. He is aware of this label and suffers from a feeling of total inadequacy. As a result of such a feeling his academic obstacles are heightened and become even greater; his frustration is relieved to some extent by 'bad' behaviour and this results in yet another label of which he is aware – and thus the self-fulfilling circuit continues!

### Teacher

The idea of the child as a pest is reinforced daily. The bad behaviour creates times of withdrawal by teachers from the normal pattern of events. Playtime is a regular source of aggravation resulting in the boy standing outside the Head's room until there is time to 'deal' with him. He therefore returns to his lessons late having missed instructions and, most importantly, the initial teaching input and he is unable to join in with activities and work patterns satisfactorily. This practice is a factor in his low level of academic achievement. The whole situation becomes impossible to resolve: the teacher is left feeling almost powerless to address any of the difficulties at all. What continues to pass unnoticed is that the child has particular academic needs which, if supported correctly, could lead to a solution of his associated behavioural needs.

### Context

At home his parents are aware of this unsympathetic climate which they feel unable to influence and yet, at the same time, they are desperately worried. They may well try to put pressure on the child, believing that he simply needs to realize that he must make more effort in all areas and an improvement will then become evident. This is not the case and parents' exasperation levels also rise. The pressure should be exerted on the school's management to evaluate the handling of this child. This is a child who does not fit the norm as he is different in some way. This makes it difficult to accommodate him. Such diversity is therefore something of a challenge for the teacher and the school.

## Creating the climate for learning

### Issues for the child

As Pollard (1996) suggests, children experience the classroom in the light of their cultural background. So teaching decisions should be balanced against knowledge of the child's previous experiences and developed skills. As diversity can come in many shapes and sizes, any decisions must be realistic and within the constraints of a large class of children.

In the classroom, collaborative pair or group work is based on children working and talking together to achieve a shared outcome (Galton and Williamson 1992). They share their experience and knowledge through the medium of language and together advance cognitively (Wood 1988; Wells 1992). The social ingredient is considered a vital one in theories of how children learn (Bruner 1996). Talk formulated when cooperating with others helps us not only to share thoughts but to shape our own thought and understanding. We suggest that in order for collaborative group work to be most effective, children who share the same levels of language should work together. If there is no shared language, then the positive effect on cognitive development will be diminshed. This suggests that it is important, if possible, to place new arrivals to Britain with children who speak their first language. This is common practice to solve communication problems until the child speaks English and is usually viewed as being for translation purposes.

We would argue that working in first language enhances cognitive development. This raises the question of who should decide the level of proficiency in English or in first language in

*Children and adults working together*

order to match children with similar skills. Qualified bilingual teachers who have knowledge of the children's first languages could make these decisions on group organization. In order for all children working together to achieve shared meanings, shared proficiency in language is also likely to be a determinant in other groupings. This raises a social class and regional dimension. One argument against grouping children on shared-language levels is that this may encourage less mixing of groups. One important benefit of collaborative group work is that it encourages children's social skills and knowledge and respect for other children (McNamara 1995). Therefore flexibility to arrange appropriate groupings is vital.

Other aspects effecting learning from collaborative work are the existing social skills that children have acquired by reason of the experiences at home. For example, an only child familiar with adult attention and participating in adult conversation, may work at a more independent level than a child from a large family. Levels of dependency found at home will vary and so the social skills required to work alone successfully or in close collaboration will differ.

The range of alternative strategies for learning that children have will also vary according to their experiences and background.

Their ability to monitor and control the use of various approaches to learning depends on 'their knowledge of the world, their perceptions of the new strategy and their expectations of success or failure' (Merry 1998: 59). Children who are encouraged to hold a questioning approach to learning at home will be more likely to question strategies at school and so become more independent learners. Those who have not been encouraged to do so will find independence harder to achieve.

When considering the youngest children in school, their experiences at home will influence their attitudes towards play-based learning activities. Play opportunities can help children explore social roles and relationships (Moyles 1989). Through such activities and the roles they have, emotions such as frustration regarding discrimination can be expressed and knowledge about the world and the different people found there will be acquired. Play can provide a vehicle for children to develop sensitivity to the feelings of others so can be an effective way of establishing positive attitudes to equality (Kitson 1994). The acknowledgement of the importance of learning achieved through play will vary in different homes, as will understanding of how children of all ages learn by active participation. Swadener and Johnson (1989) assert that parental involvement in play is shown to enhance the child's play skills. Children from families who themselves have had little experience of learning in school from a play base, may find acceptance of these activities difficult. Entry into play activities might be more tentative if children do not have the same experiences as their peers, for example a child who has not attended a pre-school facility will be approaching these opportunities in a very different way from the child who is familiar with such a situation. In homes with a high level of income, children may not be expected to contribute to household duties, leaving more time for play activities but it should be acknowledged that where children carry out a work role, the experiences gained and the skills acquired must be recognized such as those in Cameo 1 of Chapter 2. Curtis (1994) suggests that sometimes when parents tell children to 'go out and play', the child's interpretation may be that they should occupy themselves out of the parents' way, so undervaluing the play activity. So the messages children receive about play from home will influence their attitudes towards play and learning in the classroom.

### Issues for the teacher

How do the belief systems of teachers affect their teaching style?

> As teachers, we do not just act as the gateway to knowledge.
> We ourselves represent, embody, our curriculum. And, in
> our teaching, we convey not just our explicit knowledge but
> also our position towards it, the personal ramifications and
> implications which it has for us.
>
> (Salmon 1988: 12)

If some teachers have strong convictions that an understanding
of science, for example, will encourage children to conserve the
environment, and that this is a vital issue for them personally,
the science curriculum will be taught in a way which gives children messages about the importance of preserving the natural
world. The emphasis placed in the teaching of history and geography on positive perspectives of non-British societies will
depend on our view points. In planning a topic on diversity in
home life, the decision whether to present African mud huts as
the only example of the African way of life or to include houses
in capital cities is based on the individual's awareness of race and
stereotyping. Similarly, ensuring that children learn about the contribution of women in history will depend upon our own stance
on feminist issues. It is not only the content but the teaching
style that is influenced. For example, if we believe that learning
enables children to understand the world in which they live so
that they can make a contribution, this will influence the type of
climate for learning which we establish.

In order to achieve an acceptable environment for learning,
teachers may mistakenly hide away certain items in the cupboard.
These may be the values which underlie their style of teaching.
It is likely that some 'traditionalists' concealed their views post-
Plowden and followed new trends, for example, abandoning the
teaching of phonics. This would mean that the teacher did not
approach new reading methods with any enthusiasm and a resultant lack of success. The internal conflict between long-established
belief and acceptance of new ideas takes precedence over attempts
to understand the underpinning theories of any new perspective.
Openness to innovative methods is resisted. With the current
trend back towards phonics as an approach to learning to read,
these teachers will now open the cupboard (see the introduction)

and bring out their long-hidden philosophy. Of course an equal or perhaps greater, number will hide theirs away. How many feel confused and angry that their long-held beliefs are being questioned? However, there is an inner core within each person, which is defended and highly resistant to change and individuals will reject new ideas which they do not perceive to be compatible with their views of themselves in order to maintain a consistent self-concept (Rogers 1982). Nias (1989) suggests that the significance of a sense of personal identity in teaching should be understood. The job demands a massive investment of 'self'. Open debate is vital, and sufficient in-service training should be provided in a secure atmosphere to enable evaluation by each individual of current theories and practice. Stammers (1992) feels that individuals need to develop personal theories of teaching rather than just accepting a general set of principles. The school must create a climate for staff to feel safe to express opinions and give justification for their views. Action research by teacher researchers in their own classrooms is one way to keep debates healthy and positive (Elliott 1991).

The way teachers view children and make assumptions about individual's abilities influences the way they create the learning environment. Recent reports from HMI and Ofsted have expressed the belief that primary teachers generally underestimate children's abilities (Ofsted 1995, 1996b). The issue of the 'Pygmalion' or self-fulfilling prophecy has been expounded in educational literature for many years (Rosenthal and Jacobson 1968; Brophy 1983; Good 1987). This is the relationship between the teacher's expectations of the potential performance of a child based on factors such as social status, race or gender and the resulting achievement. Rosenthal and Jacobson (1968: vii) state 'how one person's expectation of another person's behaviour can quite unwittingly become a more accurate prediction simply for its having been made'. We predict (prophesy) how a person will behave and this influences our actions in relation to that person, so that the prophecy is fulfilled. If a teacher decides a particular child can only achieve at a certain level then the work is structured at that level so the achievement is unlikely to be any greater. Ayles (1996) reports on able pupils who remain unrecognized and so not catered for in classrooms. These children were especially from so-called 'disadvantaged' backgrounds or were children with a disability, where the academic ability was not as visible as the disability or the home circumstance so not addressed with appropriate work levels.

How many teacher assumptions about children in their current class are based upon knowledge of the older brothers and sisters who have previously passed through the teacher's hands? These can be both negative and positive. For example, a sister following a highly successful brother can be pressurized if not achieving at the same level. Conversely, members of large families, where several siblings have been uncooperative and underachievers, find that younger able and willing children can be labelled wrongly as 'problems'.

The factors influencing achievement are complex and simple solutions are problematic. The self-fulfilling prophecy theories have been criticized and many research projects have been instigated to investigate the claims (King 1978; Mortimore *et al.* 1988). Abbott (1996) provides an overview of the research and reports on the PACE (Primary Assessment Curriculum and Experience) project which found no evidence for a link between race, gender or class and teacher expectations. She suggests that teachers draw on many factors when assessing children including knowledge of their work and relationships. As we have seen earlier relationships in primary classrooms are complex and both the teacher and the child's view of each other are integrated with factors of personality, ability and application. Teachers are professionals who aim to use all the available knowledge of children to construct the best learning environment for each individual child.

Particularly in the area of racial identity, however, recent research has shown that teachers attitudes influence the learning context. Research reported by Mooney (1995) and Ofsted (1996a) suggests that the relationship between teachers and African-Caribbean boys can often be negative and influence professional judgements about ability, whereas Asian children are generally assumed to be well behaved, keen to learn and are treated accordingly. The negative response given to African-Caribbean boys would ensure that levels of achievement were low confirming the teacher's assumptions and perpetuating the cycle. The other children will likewise be influenced by the teacher's responses and will echo them and develop a view of the particular child as a low achiever. Weinstein (1983) found that children are aware of differences in teachers' patterns of interactions with individual children. One surprising factor used to prejudge a child's potential language development was found in the study by Ogilvy *et al.* (1990) where expectations of Asian children were based on the level of English proficiency demonstrated by the parents or older siblings. We need to examine any stereotypical assumptions still to be found in many of our schools today.

The Russian psychologist, Vygotsky, is widely recognized for his work on cognitive development (Wood 1988). He suggested that there is a 'zone of proximal development' which is the difference between a child's actual developmental level and the potential level achieved under adult or peer guidance. The crucial word here is *potential* as the adult must believe in the child's potential and therefore want to scaffold the learning. If you hold a view that the child will not be able to advance, then energetic support will not be provided and the child may not reach the 'zone of proximal development'.

### Issues for the school

It must be acknowledged that not only the teachers working in a school may come from diverse backgrounds but the other adults employed or volunteering will also represent many cultures, origins and viewpoints. The assumptions made about children and the viewpoints held about teaching and learning all affect the creation of the learning climate in the whole school.

There is now a greater emphasis on collaboration in teaching and in particular in the area of planning. This pattern of close work between teachers and support staff requires compatibility of ideas (Moyles 1997b). In a small-scale research project conducted by one of the authors (Suschitzky 1995b), it was found that individual teachers from different backgrounds often had difficulty finding common ground on pedagogical issues. However, incompatibility is possible if mutual respect is established for each other's stance and both groups are willing to listen and adapt their views. Alexander (1996: 284) states that primary practice 'requires us to try to reconcile competing values, pressures and constraints'. No teacher or other staff member should feel pressure to hide his or her philosophy in the cupboard.

An example of the need for common understanding is the school's policy of behaviour management (Docking 1996). All teachers, support staff, parents and, of course, children, need to be involved in its creation and in understanding its implementation. It is therefore vital to include lunch-time staff in equality training as Troyna and Hatcher (1992) report racist incidents often happen during free time in the lunch break. Supervisors must know how to handle these incidents. To establish effective team work the views of others must be valued. This notion will be developed in Chapter 5 as we look at ways in which to acknowledge and value the views and skills of support staff, parents and the local community.

Another example of whole-school policy formation is in dealing with such issues as countering stereotyping. The study of the Gender Equity Action Research Project (Lewis and Kellaghan 1993) concluded that teachers held stereotypical perceptions of whether boys or girls showed greater interest in certain subjects. For example, there were assumptions that boys are not interested in sewing or girls not keen on computers. The extent to which teachers perceived differences in the amount of help boys or girls need in different areas of curriculum has more implications. Ninety-three per cent of the teachers in the study thought that girls need more help in maths against 76 per cent for boys. In terms of learning styles, boys were judged to be more problem-solving and girls more collaborative and creative (Beetlestone 1998). These assumptions have great significance when creating the climate for learning. The work of teachers to counter stereotyping can be undermined if other adults in the school have not had the same opportunities to explore the issues and therefore find a consensus in working with children.

One suggestion of an awareness-raising exercise for all staff would be to examine people's assumptions held about children's names. Can stereotypical images be formed just by hearing a person's name? Adults are not always aware of their preconceived views or of the affect on children's learning of these perceptions. Do the names 'Tracey' and 'Darren' have different connotations to 'Harriet' and 'Henry'? The familiar names that children are called can be gender related as found by Browne and France (1985). Girls were called 'sweetie' and 'precious' whereas boys were called 'bruiser' and 'wise guy'. Language in this vein used in the classroom results in stereotyped notions of gender being absorbed by children. Children internalize that adults show an expectation of positive behaviour associated with girls and negative aspects with boys.

---

**ACTIVITY 4.1**

Child perception

Try this activity to examine your perceptions of the children you teach. Think of a child in your class who causes you concerns. (If you do this with a group then the gender or race of the children selected may tell you something!)

1 Make a list of his or her positive qualities and then the negative ones.
2 Which list is the longer?
3 Can you extend the positive one ?
4 How can you assist this child to succeed?

---

**STRATEGIES**

Child perception

Strategies to try would be to:

- concentrate on the positive aspects of behaviour or work (McNamara and Moreton 1995);
- let the child know that you value him or her for these things;
- give private and public recognition;
- establish a reward system for success not only for academic achievements but for displaying positive working habits and social behaviour;
- make sure that the child values the reward and establish a common agreement on this;
- make sure that the child understands the reasons for rewards and sanctions;
- aim to give responsibility for own learning or behaviour;
- ensure that all adults share the same aims for this child including support staff and volunteer parents.

---

## Equality in the climate for learning

As we have already stated, everything that happens in the class-room reflects our value system. We suggest that even the use of computers and the teaching of Information Technology (IT) are not value free activities. The attitudes towards the use of IT stem from our background, previous experience and basic value system.

---

**ACTIVITY 4.2**

**Information technology**

Read the following scenario.

> A new teacher on the staff asks the IT coordinator to show her the appropriate software for her class. When she receives a rather vague reply, she pursues this in the joint year/group planning session and inquires how much use is made of the Internet to access resources for teaching. This teacher is quickly realizing that IT use is not an integral part of teaching in her new school.

What is the basis of the enthusiastic approach to IT present in the new teacher?

What is the basis of the reluctant approach to IT present in the established teachers?

In trying to answer these questions you may have considered the following:

- teacher's level of IT skills;
- teacher's level of IT confidence;
- perceived threat by teachers of children's superior skills;
- teacher's different speed of acceptance of change;
- teacher's realization of impact of technology;
- gender factors;
- differentiation of children's home experience;
- recognition of skills learnt at home even if mainly playing games;
- recognition that a child with special education needs can succeed on a computer;
- opportunities for peer tutoring;
- recognition that computers can stretch the more able child;
- the school's policy towards IT;
- amount and appropriateness of training available;
- priority allocated to training;
- suitably qualified IT coordinator;
- skilled parental help in classroom;
- classroom organization problems caused by a single computer per class;
- lack of appropriate equipment;
- lack of maintenance of equipment;

---

- school priorities for budgeting for IT;
- level of parent–teacher association fund raising for equipment.

This long list (you may feel able to add more aspects) demonstrates that all our actions in the primary classroom are complex and are influenced by both our own backgrounds and ideology as well as the stance held by colleagues, parents and local and central government representatives.

## Conclusion

It is our responsibility as teachers to prepare *all* children for the future, so we must recognize that acceptance or rejection of teaching methods or a teaching emphasis is based on our own value system. Each school community must decide how it is going to create the climate for learning. The method employed may be to leave each individual teacher to follow his or her own teaching beliefs or to impose a strict prescriptive system of planning, lesson delivery and organization. For most schools, the solution will be to try to arrive at a consensus of views. As described in Chapter 1, the elements that make up the identity of a school influence the creation of the ethos found there.

There needs to be an acceptance of different ways of learning and perceptions of teaching. In order for a suitable climate for learning to be encouraged, teachers needs to recognize that diversity is, of itself, a 'norm' and to empathize with the special requirements it will present as well as use constructively the special dimensions it brings.

Shaw wrote *Pygmalion* in 1913 and Rosenthal and Jacobson used this quote to close their book in 1968 but it is still true today at the close of the twentieth century.

You see, really and truly, apart from the things that anyone can pick up . . . the difference between a lady and a flower girl is not how she behaves but how she is treated.

(George Bernard Shaw)

The challenge of education in the twenty-first century is to value both ways of life, that of the lady and that of the flower girl and for everyone to learn from both.

It should never be forgotten that children thrive when they have a sense of ownership of the learning (Pollard 1996), so they need to be a part of the process of decisions about teaching methods. This can only be achieved if a relationship is established between learner and teacher that encourages understanding and respect for this process. In Chapter 5 we will turn to the influence of the home and community on the learning scenario and how we can find ways to hold the experience, knowledge and skills of the children, and their homes and communities, in high regard.

**5**

# Home and community influence: who passes through the gate?

**Cameo 1**

Dear Ann

The new house is great but we can't decide which school to send the kids to. The estate agent said that everyone moves here because the village school is high in the league tables but the neighbours send their children to the school in the next village because they don't like mixed ability teaching. I have made a brief visit to both schools and got their brochures, but what do they mean by a 'child-centred approach' and 'whole-class interactive teaching methods?' How am I supposed to know which are progressive or traditional methods and where I can read the Ofsted reports? It is such an important decision.

**Cameo 2**

In the staffroom over lunch, the Reception class teacher, Gwyneth Rosser, is retelling the following incident:
'Can you guess which of my new entrants has not got any PE shoes? Yes, you're right, Victor James. I remember his two brothers never had any either. So I decided he is not allowed to do PE until he gets some. I'm surprised you didn't hear his Mum coming down the corridor. She came storming into the classroom to complain. She was shouting like a fishwife and yelled that she was going to take action as her child was entitled to PE lessons. How am I supposed to gain respect from the new children with parents like that?'

## Introduction

No chapter, concerned with the influence of the home on children's learning, can begin without first acknowledging that parents are a child's first educators and that they continue to be the prime influence even after the child has started school. The type of community in which the home is situated will also greatly influence the child's education. So home–school links should always be considered in conjunction with community links.

Even though the deficit view of parenting prevalent before the 1970s has diminished (Bernstein 1971; Tough 1977) an underlying view of parents as somehow 'lacking' can still be found in primary schools today. This negative view can take the form of criticizing lower-income families for not providing stimulation for children or of higher-income families for not giving children independence. Hughes (1989: 149) found reception teachers reported that, in their view, children entered school with nothing at all and they were not prepared to look for any already developed competencies. Do teachers today regard the home as a powerful learning environment or as Hughes found 'a strong negative influence against which they were constantly battling'? This chapter recognizes that many teachers do work hard towards positive parental involvement and will raise issues to suggest extension of this commitment.

At the same time as recognizing that there is much commonality to be found in the home experiences of different children, and that groupings can be made, this chapter will emphasize the uniqueness of each child's experience (Ferris 1997) and attempt to avoid describing stereotypical behaviour. While acknowledging the varied family contexts in which children live today, we will use the term 'parents' to represent those who care for and hold prime responsibility for the child as defined in The Children Act (Department of Health 1989).

## Principles of working with parents

To examine ways to create an ethos where children, parents and community are valued and equally one where teachers feel valued, we will first consider four principles suggested by Wolfendale (1992: 3) for working with parents: rights, equality, reciprocity and empowerment.

## Rights

Parents have fundamental rights to be involved in some educational decision making as enshrined in the Education Reform Act 1988. But government's stance of giving more parent power assumes that parents are a 'national homogeneous entity' (Mac An Ghaill 1995). Social group, gender and ethnic origin may, however, determine the way that parents can respond to the power given. The questions to be raised are whether governing bodies reflect the local area and the ethnic and socio-economic make up of the parents in that area and whether all parents have access to governors. Hatcher *et al.* (1996) report on low involvement of Asian parents in school activities because of language barriers, work commitment and lack of confidence in a white-dominated environment. There must be channels available for all parents to feel empowered and able to contribute to the work of the school in order for them to exercise their basic rights.

## Equality

In this sense, equality means equal status between parents and professionals acknowledging different but equivalent experience and expertise. This raises questions such as who decides what expertise is acceptable and on what terms is experience measured and so deemed valuable. We believe that if there is an ethos in the school of valuing all skills and experience, then this will provide a climate of equality. Children will then receive messages that their family and community are accepted on an equal level.

## Reciprocity

Each person is involved in contributing and sharing and each stands to gain but that accountability belongs to all. Teachers believe that they can make a positive difference to children's lives but they must believe that parents can too. Reciprocity can be best achieved by a 'large table approach' (Vasconcelos 1997), which involves all partners in true conversation with everyone around the table with equal say to negotiate and present opinions and contributions.

If a partnership between parents and staff is present then all should take a part in school evaluation and goal setting for future effectiveness. This also means that accountability has to be taken

by all and a support network established. We make further suggestions on how to involve everyone in determining a common
framework for education in Chapter 6.

### Empowerment

Parental involvement should provide opportunities for parents
to grow sufficiently confident to work within the system and be
able to challenge existing structures. Empowering parents means
that teachers must accept that this will enable parents to carry
out actions that may go against cherished educational principles.
For example, headteachers who do not instigate certain policies,
which are favoured by parents with a strong representation on
the governing body, may find that their salary is not raised or
even that a climate is created whereby resignation becomes a
desired option.

### Knowledge of community and the community's knowledge of the school

Cameo 1 is concerned with the parents' view of their child's
teacher and the school. Faltis (1993) recommends that a partnership
can be established by teachers finding out about the home environment of their pupils and parents finding out about the school.

### Child

In many respects, the child here is playing a strangely passive
role. His parents have moved him from the house and environment with which he was familiar; they have broken up his daily
friendship groups; they are now in the process of searching for a
school which they consider will be appropriate to fulfill his academic needs. In many ways he is rather like a counter in a game,
something to be placed – not according to his wishes but in
accordance with the supposed wisdom of his carers. In many
homes, he will be a part of important discussions and decision-
making. But in the final instance he will have to be content with
that which is decided for him.

Moreover, although his involvement in the original decisions
may be small the overall effect on his life will be enormous: it
will influence his academic achievements; it will dictate to a large

extent his social contacts; it will mould his personality in ways which may direct the rest of his life. What an overwhelming realization!

## Teacher

In many respects, the role of the teacher in Cameo 1 is also a passive one: he or she is being viewed initially from a distance and perhaps from official documentary evidence in the form of Ofsted reports and league tables, coupled with hearsay collated by the parents from new neighbours and the local community. There will, in fact, be a received collection of opinions based on various different perceptions.

Alongside will, at some point, be a meeting between the parents and the headteacher and maybe an introduction to other members of staff. It is at this point in the process that a teacher may be able to present views and aspirations for those children for whom she or he has responsibility. But, in most contexts, it is unlikely to be a lengthy meeting. Pressures on time are great and it is likely that after a brief conversation the parents will return home with the school's official brochure.

## Context

It is really the parents who provide the focus of the context here. They are attempting to evaluate a school and match it with the needs of their child and their personal aspirations for the child. Their evaluations will necessarily be influenced by their own personal views. What they consider to be of importance in education and the ethos of a school will override other factors. Their own personal experiences will necessarily have helped to form their opinions. So they are coming with a set of expectations.

Nevertheless, this will also be influenced by the received information they have, both formal and unofficial, and this will inform their ultimate choice. From where does the unofficial knowledge come? The majority of the information is from other parents talking at the school gate and of course, the children's own report of the day in school. But how do parents interpret the frequent child response of 'we did nothing today?' Moreover, there is the hidden ethos of the school. But how much of this is revealed on an introductory visit is open to conjecture. For many parents, who do not have an educational field as their background, collecting the right type of information will be an exacting challenge. Coupled with the educational jargon which may be presented to them at different points, the whole process may be quite frightening. For example, when the term 'active learning' is used or 'independent learning', it may be assumed that the parent understands the significance in terms of their child's education but the opposite may in fact be true.

Can the criteria for evaluating the school change as the child progresses through the school? The answer is surely yes. In the early years, concern is with the contentment of the child at school and later the focus may change to a concern with the rate of academic progress and achieving parity with the peer group.

The expectations of parents at the beginning may be moulded by the dialogue which develops between the parent and the school so that questions raised by the young parent in the cameo should have been answered during the child's time at the school. What has then in fact happened is that the involvement of the parent in school matters has developed and resulted in effective partnership.

## Influence of home balanced against that of school

### Child

Victor in Cameo 2 is in the old role of 'piggy in the middle'. On one side is his mother who is a major figure in his life. Her role is almost impossible to define for homes and relationships are as varied as the pebbles on the seashore. But it is probably safe to assume that she is important – and this could be in a variety of ways. She may provide strong emotional support; practical skills to enable the everyday life to continue; financial means to feed and clothe; friendship and fun. Above all she is the pivot upon which his life revolves.

But on the other side is Mrs Rosser – a newer influence. Within the school environment she holds power: she makes decisions which continually affect his school experience; she directs his activities; she praises and scolds; she tells his parents what he has been doing.

Victor will soon assess that there are two differing positions of power here. But also he will soon make the correct assessment that in order to survive successfully it is imperative that he gives allegiance to both. The question of when is usually decided for him by the situation. However, in this particular case, a conflict has arisen by them both requiring allegiance at the same time in totally different ways.

## Teacher

It is apparent from some of Gwyneth Rosser's remarks that views already formed about the James family are being projected on to Victor. It is likely that certain patterns of behaviour and certain responses are expected already both from him and his mother. As Mrs Rosser experiences this verbal attack from a parent in front of the children which is also overheard by colleagues, she will feel both angry and threatened and also that her status as a teacher is undermined.

It is therefore essential that she seeks to find a middle ground from which to operate successfully so that parent and teacher can start communicating effectively. An opportunity must be arranged for an honest exchange of views where each person is respected equally.

## Context

The scenario illustrates the undervaluing that has taken place in the status and authority of teachers in society's view over the years. Victor's family do not shy away from criticizing his teacher in public. Schools have to work in a climate whereby respect from home and community has to be earned. The staff have to work with parents to achieve reciprocity as advocated in the principles of working with parents suggested on page 83. There should be a framework within the school for teachers to be able to deal with this situation, so that when it occurs they know exactly what to do and that the policy has been agreed upon. However, it is imperative that positive ways of working together are sought. Parents need to feel that there is a place where their views can be expressed and valued. Teachers equally need to feel that they are being adequately supported. The final goal must inevitably be that of forming a partnership in which both can operate effectively and happily. Achieving this will require careful planning over a long time by all staff and parents.

## The influence of home and community

### Issues for the child

*Significant people in children's lives*

Who are the people who are most significant in a child's life and over which of the child's feelings and behaviour patterns do they hold influence? As teachers, we need to have some awareness of these influences and recognize that such people in children's lives will vary greatly according to family structure and cultural or religious emphasis. For example, it cannot be assumed that parents hold the most control over the child at home. In extended families, the traditional respect accorded to grandparents will be a significant influence on the child's behaviour. When a parent has to leave the child with other carers for substantial periods of time, this may result in the following instruction to the child 'Do exactly as Grandma/Uncle Jim/big sister says until I come home'. Also, we cannot assume that any particular family member will be influential as different children will respond to significant people in different ways according to their inner feelings. The amount of influence will also change over time as the child matures and receives greater influence from peers or outsiders or the family context undergoes a substantial change.

Edwards and Knight (1994) report on research that found that young children could discriminate between the behaviour allowed at home and that found in school settings. This means that children learn how to cope with differing codes and balance their behaviour accordingly. But does any one set of rules hold a stronger influence over the child's actions than any other? The answer will be dependent on the individual's personality, the strength and commitment of the family and the status that education is accorded within that family.

*Implications for practitioners working with children
in the classroom: attitudes to learning*

The child will respond to the expectations in educational terms of these significant people. The valuing or undervaluing of educational achievement found in the home or community will affect the child's attitude to learning. In families where education

**ACTIVITY 5.1**

**Influences on children's lives**

In order to understand the variety of influences on children's lives you might try the following.

Take three children that you know well and draw an ecosystem for each one. An ecosystem is concerned with the relationship of living organisms to their surroundings and other members who live there. Ecosystems are not static and for a child this may change frequently. Draw a large circle Place a small circle for the child in the centre and draw other circles to represent significant people in the child's life.

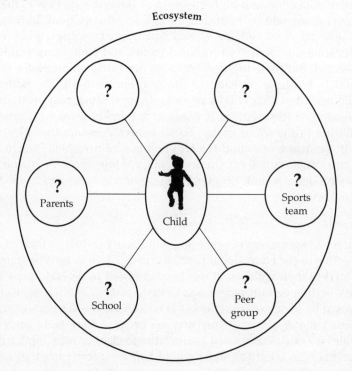

Ecosystem

*Figure 5.1*

Where are the most circles? Are there any overlaps?

What does this tell you about the major influences to be found on the children in the school?

at a higher level is not a common experience, then education is often viewed as a privilege. The child may be encouraged to work hard and value the experience showing respect for the education system. In traditional working-class communities, education was seen as a means to an end and that qualifications would ensure a good job. But with the decline in traditional manufacturing industries and the changes to working patterns a 'good education' does not now necessarily lead to work security. Children are growing up in areas of high unemployment where there are few role models of working people. This means that these children have very little to which they can aspire and this is likely to be reflected in their attitude to learning in school. In families where education at a higher level is a common experience, then expectations will be high that the child will gain qualifications. Family activities will be geared towards extending children's education and books, educational games and computers will be plentiful. But these high expectations can bring problems for the child in terms of pressure to succeed. For example, the parent who describes their child's work as disappointing, may really be referring to the fact that it is not at a parallel level with other children in the social group. Social expectations are interwoven with academic ones and the two become inseparable. The child in this situation will experience feelings of low self-esteem which may hinder academic progress, causing nervousness and inability to achieve.

*Parents' own educational experiences*

Parents' experiences of schooling will greatly influence their perspective of the educational process and this will in turn be transmitted to their children. It can be manifested in several forms. It may be that certain parents, as Connell *et al.* (1982) found, were injured by their own experiences at school and this disempowered them later as parents. This may be because they were underachievers or discriminated against due to class or race. Similarly, parents who went to public school had an upbringing that can strongly affect their views of education. A parent used to an authoritarian teaching style and an expected high level of success would convey to their child a strong sense of failure if they did not attain expected results.

Many parents have experience of a more formal education than that found in primary schools today. If this was in schools where emphasis was placed on product rather than on processes, then understanding the style of learning encouraged for their child may be difficult and the child will be caught in the middle between two perspectives. For example, the parent will expect the work to be marked rigorously and that the child will get everything right, resulting in pressure on the child to produce correctly written work every time.

Another difference may be in terms of an uneven value placed on certain aspects of curriculum. For example, comments such as the following are frequently heard:

'It's a waste of time to study art and music when maths is so important.'

'I could never do maths and I've survived.'

'History is boring and no use after you have left school.'

What messages do these give to children?

If there is a difference between home and school perspectives on the cause of low attainment, this could produce a dilemma for the child. In some cultures, the reason for low levels of achievement would be attributed to a lack of work, which can be remedied by striving harder. However, a more British approach may be to suggest that the child cannot succeed at a higher rate as she or he is 'not clever enough' (Biggs 1994). On the one hand, the family may believe that failure can be corrected by more and more effort but the school may believe that the child does not have the ability to raise the level of achievement. This mismatch could result in pressure from the parents for the child to attend private tuition and to spend long hours in extra work while the school may not stretch the child at all.

## Issues for the teacher

If teachers are going to meet the needs of all children in their care then they must have some understanding of the expectations and views of schooling occurring in the children's home and community.

### Establishing the relationship with parents

Establishing and maintaining good relationships with parents requires careful consideration. Parents' views about what constitutes an acceptable relationship between families and schools will be influenced by their experiences, which may be of a system where the relationship is formal and socially distant (see Bastiani 1997). Some parents have been brought up to hold teachers at a respectful distance. There must be some cultural shock for parents to be greeted by nursery or reception teachers and even headteachers in very informal ways, who with well meaning intentions try to convey that school is an informal and open place.

Teachers have to balance, on the one hand, being the paid qualified person responsible for the education of children, with the professional who wishes to share the educational role. In most schools, the teacher assumes the role of dominant partner as the educated person, but in middle-class areas parents can be so assertive that they control the relationship. At its extreme, parent governors are able to put so much pressure on a headteacher who does not meet community expectations that eventually the head may leave the school through stress related illness or take early retirement.

Having to deal with the high expectations of middle-class parents who constantly monitor their child's progress can be threatening as the teacher feels that every move is watched and they are accountable for every action. But teachers are accountable for their work and both parties will feel secure if a partnership with parents is established where honesty and openness is present.

When working with ethnic minority parents, teachers must address their rising expectations that their children are to be equipped to compete equally for further and higher education places. Classroom practice should be examined to ensure that it does not disadvantage ethnic minority children by undervaluing their skills and experience or by use of eurocentric teaching materials.

*Giving feedback on children's progress*

Where the learning is differentiated mainly by outcome, the feedback provided by teachers also has to be differentiated. Children and parents may easily interpret different feedback given by teachers on children's progress incorrectly. Ofsted (1995) found that many reports to parents are unduly positive and fail to make constructive criticism. There should be a difference between constructive reporting and undue positive reporting. For example, Miss Brown is working with her class on a creative writing piece. Her aim for Tom is for five correctly spelt sentences and she will give profuse praise if this is achieved, but for James she will only use the word 'good' if two pages of imaginative, expressive work are presented. Miss Brown has very good reasons for the difference but the children may well not understand. Children soon learn the hierarchy of the classroom but they can rarely adequately read teachers' minds and fully comprehend expectations for individual children. The children's experience of the use of praise at home, such as frequency of use and on what occasions, will depend on the family and its priorities. Perhaps football skills receive more praise than writing abilities. Some children may frequently be praised by family members for their accomplishments. Teachers who are trying to adopt positive behaviour management strategies may find that the praise given to such children falls on 'deaf ears'. But children, who do not experience such a warm environment of praise at home, may respond more enthusiastically to a positive approach and therefore the strategy has greater effect. It makes the process more genuine when teachers receive a welcoming response.

This differentiation of giving feedback is then continued when reporting to parents takes place. When we give parents a positive picture of their child, do we provide this in the context of the rest of the class and the wider school population? If we tell Tom's parents that he is doing well but he only achieves Level 2 when the Key Stage 2 SATs are reported, we may not have provided sufficient information for them to set realistic expectations for their son's future. Parents need a clear idea about how their children are progressing and in what ways. It is vital to report to parents on the whole child achieving a balance between the academic and the creative and social skills. However, because society gives such credit to academic success, teachers have a responsibility to present a true picture of this aspect of a child but also to help parents to see where the potential of children's talents in the arts, sports, social and organizational domains may lead. If culturally parents are more used to criticism being blunt and not couched in positive terms, there will be misunderstandings over the terminology used and parents may experience difficulty knowing their child's level.

Many schools have developed the use of a record of achievement for each pupil. The child usually is involved in the selection of its content (Johnson *et al.* 1992). Schools must ensure that parents understand the purpose of records of achievement and the process that is involved in its creation. If parents have no experience from their own schooling or work environment of being part of self-assessment, then they may not appreciate the child's role in assessment.

## Issues for the school

*Parental involvement: do the parents and community pass easily through the school gate?*

Parental involvement in the school aspect of their children's education is now held by both schools and parents to be beneficial (Ball 1994). Bastiani (1997) suggests that parental involvement is now seen by schools as an important ingredient in school effectiveness and the raising of pupil achievement. But the extent and commitment of schools can vary enormously and whether there is consensus within the teaching profession about understanding and interpreting this concept is debatable. We need to consider exactly what we mean by the term 'parental involvement'. Involvement of parents in the education of primary children can be perceived at various levels. One level that is common to most schools is *direct communication with teacher*. The parent's role is threefold:

- Provider of information about child.
- Receiver of information about child.
- Problem solver.

Another level is *active involvement,* where the role is as a pair of hands or as a fund raiser. Both are important aspects of school participation. However, these two levels are often the only ones found in schools. But a further level of involvement is that of *partner in children's learning.* This is where there is a frequent dialogue between parent and teacher with joint decisions and action. The parents' role at this level is very different from the first two. Of course, parents are also involved in *school management,* where the role is one of elected member of the governing body. Many schools also see the *development of parents* as an important element of encouraging involvement. The school then becomes a provider of community education with the parent as participant.

Edwards and Knight (1997) state that what determines the nature of the parent–school relationship is found in the aims of the school. This suggests that a school with an ethos of valuing the contributions of all and emphasizing the acceptance of diversity, will be one that views parents as partners in children's education. This is confirmed by Bastiani (1997: 17) who suggests that the 'underlying attitudes and positive practice are just as influential as matters of structure and organisation in determining whether or not home–school work in multicultural settings is effective'. The allocation of time for teachers to communicate with parents, is one example where the underlying ethos can effect the school's structure. If a policy is developed giving importance to discussions with parents, structures will be established to ensure that time is allocated. Priority given to this may well mean that other issues are not covered. Putting policies into practice is not always easy.

As Atkin and Bastiani (1988) state, an important element of a parent-centred philosophy is respect for the everyday lives of ordinary people for its own sake. This requires that teachers have knowledge of the lives of the families that attend the school.

It is the responsibility of the school management to provide the time for teachers to listen to parents and act upon the information gathered. In order to improve direct communication with parents, home–school liaison work is well established in many areas. This is, however, more frequently found in areas of high social disadvantage, where there is a perceived view that more parental involvement will increase attainment. Often home–school liaison work is provided by Section 11 funding, which was given to meet the specific needs of bilingual pupils and ensure equal access to the curriculum. This is not a mainstream provision and so signifies a reluctance by schools to give this work a high priority. The service provided by Section 11 staff is often seen as solving problems, i.e. the parents do not speak English and we (the teachers) do not understand their culture. The response to any perceived difficulty is therefore to send round the bilingual home–school officer. Questions must be raised about the status of these staff within the school structure and the use of the information provided by their visits to children's homes. The undervaluing of such work can create as many problems as solutions.

*Community involvement: do the teachers and children go out through the gates to the community?*

A school cannot operate in isolation from its local environment. Knowledge of the locality can strengthen the school's capacity to enhance children's learning. Thomas (1985) asserts that learning is effective when it draws upon a range of experiences wider than that provided by the school. Many schools include 'community participation' in their aims but the interpretation of this can be as varied as the interpretation of parental involvement.

As with parental involvement, so extending the community life of the school is seen as good practice. But what exactly do we mean by community involvement?

---

**ACTIVITY 5.2**

**Food for thought**

You may like to try and write down a definition of 'Community'. It would be interesting to ask two or three people from within and outside of school to do the same and to compare statements. People's definitions will vary according to their perspective of community living.

Another item to consider is the limits of the 'community'. We frequently only think in terms of the geographical area surrounding the school. But wherever the child interacts on a regular basis may be deemed its community. If the family has strong links with their origins in Scotland or Bangladesh, then the child's sense of community will be extensive. If the family partakes of certain activities, then members of the town's choir or fishing club will be part of that child's community as well.

It is not enough just to have knowledge about the environment in which the children live. The important factor is what we do with our acquired knowledge. Teachers must understand the realities of the immediate environment by acknowledging the constraints, concerns and aspirations of the community and demonstrating that this way of life is valued and respected. If we view the locality of the school in a negative way and feel that the school must 'compensate' for the poor living conditions of the children, then we are missing an opportunity to foster pride in children about their environment.

Sweeping statements about the local community need to be avoided as it must be recognized that any one community may not have a common feeling of belonging and group solidarity. There may be a multitude of groupings that are formed by people who wish to share similar interests (Antonouris and Wilson 1989).

**Profiling**

---

**STRATEGIES**

Profiles

One method to provide a positive view of the child and his or her background is to compile a profile of each child. An element of this record should be relevant information about the child's home background. But for this to be meaningful, several questions must be raised. What should be collected? How will this be carried out? Who will be involved in the process? Ackers (1994) suggests that profiling must be a whole-school process requiring a positive lead by school management and provision for staff training.

---

**What shall I collect?**

A profile could contain four aspects:

1 Information about the child's identity.
2 A baseline assessment.
3 A description of the child's development.
4 A celebration of the child's achievements.

Background information about all aspects of a child's identity, as described in Chapter 1, should be included. But this should be recorded in an objective way without value statements. Cameo 2 (page 81) shows how easily negative statements about family values can be made. The information recorded should really inform the learning process.

**Who will contribute?**

Ritchie (1991) suggests that parental involvement in the formation of the profile is essential and that it should be a dialogue between parent, teacher and child. Parents have an intimate working knowledge of their child in contexts that are different from that of the school (Harding and Meldon-Smith 1996). The child's contribution in selecting materials for inclusion must also be valued. It is most important to find out how the child sees itself and acknowledge this. For example, do not call a child black if their skin colour is brown.

In order to obtain accurate information, ask parents how they describe their children's identity. This is especially important if the child has a dual heritage as schools must be sensitive to the child's need for a clear identity. Do not make the assumption that because the family is Punjabi they will follow the Sikh religion or that the home language is Punjabi. There needs to be an on going dialogue with the parent so that changes in circumstances are recorded. This information may be the most vital but not always the easiest for the parent to report. Two ingredients are necessary for this to be effective:

1 The parent must understand the effect on the child's welfare and learning if the teacher has information.
2 There is a mechanism for giving this in a sensitive and non-threatening way and security that confidentiality will be maintained.

Teachers are aware of sensitive issues but it is sometimes difficult to handle them. In some cultures families do not want to lose face and therefore will not 'wash their dirty linen in public'. Parents should feel that they do not need to hide away information in the cupboard. In order to create the climate whereby this happens, there must be mutual respect, open dialogue and healthy debate. A check for value judgements made on statements recorded can be made by asking if the statement is objective, if the statement is positive, if the information is really needed for the purpose intended. Observations made in the classroom of children learning can then be used to confirm our initial opinions.

### How will you collect the information?

Home visits may be an appropriate method to do this. Early years' practitioners regularly make home visits before a child's entry to school (Moyles and Suschitzky 1994). We would suggest that home visiting by staff, who teach the older year groups, would be beneficial. If the purpose for making home visits in the nursery is to gather information about the home in order to inform the provision of appropriate learning activities, this needs to be updated regularly and made relevant to older children's learning. The time and organizational implications of this are, of course, enormous. Home–school liaison staff perform this task but as previously mentioned this resource is not universally available and the information gathered must be related to the specific purpose. Within year-group team management, consideration could be given to a rolling programme of visiting.

We must, however, raise questions such as whether a home visit would confirm any stereotypical attitudes held or whether it would encourage low level expectations of the child or unrealistically high ones.

## Work with parents in school

The establishment of family literacy work is a recent innovation in many primary schools, which tries to counter the downward spiral of underachievement and lack of self-esteem found in some communities. By extending the reading skills of parents in conjunction with teaching children to read, the projects aim to work across generations and improve the literacy levels of all the family (Wolfendale and Topping 1996).

When considering issues, such as homework for primary children and implementation of home–school contracts, we should take account of the constraints under which the family operates. But circumstances in homes must be viewed from varying perspectives. For example, the fact that there is no available quiet room for work, may mean that some children are disadvantaged but other children, brought up in noisy places, may not be distracted by loud music or the presence of family members.

---

**ACTIVITY 5.3**

**Using the community as a resource**

The local area and the experiences and skills of the people that live there can be a valuable resource for schools to use.
   Try a positive approach:

1 What knowledge do you have of the support services available to the local community?
2 Can you foster partnerships with other agencies who provide support to families?
3 What can the community offer as a learning resource to the school? This can be in business, arts, culture, environment, languages, transport systems, or even produce found in local shops.

Take each area of the curriculum in turn. What aspects can be enhanced by:

1 making a visit into the community;
2 by inviting someone in to speak to the class;
3 by requesting information or resources that can be used.

*Example: Music*

1 Take children to listen to the musicians at the local church, temple or synagogue.
2 Ask for volunteers from the local choral society to assist with singing.
3 Use tapes of a local rock band's music.
4 Make cross-curricular links with religious education, science, speaking and listening.

If teachers see the value of using the community to enhance the teaching of the curriculum, this will raise the esteem of the community in the teacher's eyes which in turn will send messages to children that their background is valued. Children should feel proud of their local community and want to be a part of it and not hide their background in the cupboard.

When parents and other community members from varied backgrounds come into school, the children receive messages that these people are valued. The children hear varied uses of language, and in some areas, different national languages spoken, which helps to widen experience and counter racism. There are opportunities to counter gender stereotyping when children see people with skills and abilities that are not gender specific such as fathers cooking and mothers helping with computer work. People can be invited into school as experts with something to contribute to children's learning so raising community esteem.

Encourage the children to write about their community. Research for this will help them see the positive aspects of the area. One approach would be to encourage the class to go out and interview local people and make a local newspaper or if possible a video. The selection of people, buildings and events will enhance their view about the area.

## Conclusion

There is a South African saying that it takes a whole village to educate a child. It must be remembered that a child is always part of a larger community and no individual stands on his or her own ground; it is always shared ground. The young child initially learns to share the ground with its immediate family and nearby community. Then this expands to include a much larger group including the family of the school. Children are acquiring responsibilities to those around them just as much as these people have responsibilities for the children. Perhaps we should strive to use the local 'village' to help a school educate its children. In our last chapter, Chapter 6, we will examine the balancing of responsibilities for children and teachers and all those involved in primary education.

# 6
# Responsibilities and realities: the insurance policy

**Cameo 1**

One Saturday morning, Margaret Smith, an early years teacher, picks up the *Daily Mail* and reads the following headline: 5-YEAR-OLDS TO GET GAY LESSONS. The rest of the front page is taken up by a vitriolic piece about teachers promoting homosexuality to young children. Also on her breakfast table is the *Times Educational Supplement*, in which an article reporting the publication of a teacher's resource book on homosexuality is found. The author of the article discusses the issues in a professional way, suggesting that teachers have a responsibility to provide positive images for young children and to discuss alternative family couplings. While she is considering her feelings about these two different approaches to this educational issue, her neighbour calls round and she finds that she must comment on the tabloid's headline (Whitehead 1996a; *Daily Mail* 1996).

**Cameo 2**

St Luke's Primary School is adapting its reading policy in line with new government initiatives on literacy and parental involvement. Teachers feel it is imperative that parents understand their role so a series of parents' meetings has been arranged to explain the policy. The headteacher has invited a visiting speaker and all the staff will be present. Fatima, a Muslim child, who is from one of the 20 Muslim families in the school, reports to her teacher that her parents cannot attend because it is Ramadan and the family will be breaking their fast at that time. A management decision was then made not to change the date of the arranged meetings but to arrange a separate session for the Muslim parents with the home school liaison officer, who would explain the policy to them.

## Introduction

In the very first cameo in the Introduction to this book (page 1), we narrated the story of the teachers who felt that important objects should be stored safely away. In this last chapter, we will examine ways to protect the things that are important to children and teachers. A common practice in many cultures is to take out an insurance policy, which protects our most valuable possessions. In order to do this, we first list them and try to place a value on them. But there must be agreement with the Insurance Company about the value of each item. When we begin to look at primary education then a similar process should operate. There must be a commonly agreed mechanism for valuations. As teachers (the clients) we must justify to the public (insurance company) our reasons for wanting to protect these valuable items. But what are we insuring against? The risks in the field of education are not fire, flood and acts of God but pressure from central government, local agendas, power relationships, conformity, emphasis on outcomes only and lack of knowledge. As Alexander (1997) states, good primary practice requires that we reconcile competing values, pressures and constraints. Primary teaching is like trying to juggle with three balls in the air at once (see Figure 6.1).

As teachers, we have responsibilities to ourselves, to education and to the wider society. This means that we attempt to meet individual needs, demands of pedagogy and demands of society's value system. This interface of issues concerning the child, the teacher and the context has been the theme of this book and of all the books in this series. In this final chapter, we will consider how to balance the responsibilities of being an individual, a member of a school, and a member of the wider society, and we will try to establish mechanisms for agreement on what is to be valued and so protected.

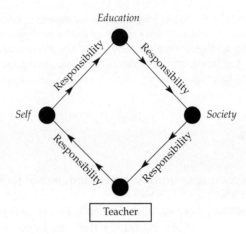

*Figure 6.1*

## Balancing personal, educational and society's perspectives

### Child

Children will have knowledge of the diversity of relationships which exist either via the TV, magazines or by personal contact, as for example, when a young child who has an elder sibling who has 'come out', so declaring their homosexuality. As the headline in Cameo 1 shows, such media stories are value-laden. We need to ensure that children understand that there are a range of acceptable lifestyles and to portray positive images of diverse relationships in order to counter homophobic attitudes. The child, who is cared for by two gay people in a permanent relationship, needs to be allowed to be open about their family lifestyle and for it to be accepted by the school community, in the same way that the child with a gay brother or sister needs to be able to retain love and respect for that sibling.

### Teacher

Margaret is torn between her professional obligation and the response of the media. The influence of family and friends may cause her to make a stance for or against the profession and her own personal view of this sensitive issue is challenged. In many ways, the neighbour represents what society might think and say. As there is confusion in people's responses on the subject of lesbian and gay issues (Epstein 1994), teachers are often expected to give a lead. Margaret must justify one way or other how she will respond in the classroom. It is essential that she examines her own views and emotions because it is only when she has successfully dealt with those that she will be able to address situations in respect to children: for example, how she will respond to the child, already mentioned, who announces that her older brother has 'come out'. We would suggest that the child is encouraged to talk about this, but mainly in terms of describing actual family events so that the teacher's responses can be objective and without value judgements.

## Context

In response to the heated public debate concerning gay rights in the 1980s, the Government issued Section 28 of the Local Government Act 1988, which prohibited the promotion of homosexuality by local authorities. This has not been enforced and as school governors are responsible for sex education there is a lack of clarity on this issue. By 1996, it was assumed that public opinion had moved. However, as the newspaper headline in cameo 1 demonstrates, there is still much public debate to take place. The question can be raised as to why there is a requirement to have a named governor for sex education but not for National Curriculum subjects such as English. This may be because there are issues concerning sex education that cause concerns for parents and society as a whole but the teaching of English is regarded as within the teacher's domain. Discussions of sex education and sexuality issues attract controversy and a small incident can be quickly blown up by the local and even national press. Governors are, of course, responsible for the English curriculum but here there are statutory programmes of study for teachers to follow. This issue would perhaps only be placed on the agenda for discussions at staff and governors meetings if there had been a situation which required a response. As with many equality issues, the adage 'no problem here' ensures that ways to counter prejudice are not even discussed let alone strategies formulated and implemented.

The situation presented in Cameo 1 required Margaret to resolve:

1  her own personal stance;
2  work within school policies and educational views;
3  ways to present and justify this view to people outside of education.

## Acknowledging the needs of the minority within the majority

### Child

Fatima, in Cameo 2, feels embarrassed that her parents cannot conform with the teacher's request especially as she holds her teacher in great esteem. She has some hidden fears that the teacher may in future think less of her because her parents have not attended an important event. However, she is well aware of the requirements of her Muslim life and the importance of the fast during Ramadan. The situation presents a conflict between her family and her religious responsibilities and those of her teacher and school.

### Teacher

The teacher is surprised by the fact that the parents cannot attend the meeting as she has not taken into account the religious occasion. Within school, she has always acknowledged diversity but finds this situation an embarrassment as it interferes with the school's educational plan. She needs to refer the matter to the school management team and will no doubt find that other teachers have met similar responses. She will have a view point as to whether to change the date of the meeting or accept that some parents will be absent. She may, however, decide to leave this difficult decision to a higher level.

## Context

Management's response to the situation may be to deal quickly without discussion, as happened in the Cameo or to arrange a meeting of parents, teachers and governors to discuss the underlying issues of this scenario. The staff in the Cameo feel that they have solved the situation as they feel that they cannot change the timetable just for a few parents. The question to be asked is how many parents does it take before changes are made? The school's action means that access to a new educational initiative, designed to improve literacy, has been denied to some parents. The arrangement of a session with only the home–school liaison officer is a token towards equality but in fact results in inequality. This group of children may well be disadvantaged in their development of literacy skills. In a nationwide survey, Ofsted (1996a) report that Muslim children fare less well academically than children from other ethnic groups. It can be conjectured that the situation may have been different if the parents were not Muslim and the reason for the difficulty was not a religious one.

## Pressures and responsibilities

### Personal responsibilities for children and teachers

Both the child and the teacher have responsibilities to their own individual identity. However, being proud of one's identity can be difficult in a world that uses the rhetoric of equality but does not always follow it in reality. If certain sections of the wider society hold a negative view of one or more elements of identity, then the reality for the child may be denial or confusion. For example, we have been told of black children who have been known to try and scrub their skin to make it white. For the bilingual child, the first language may be accepted on a superficial level but praise is more frequently given for skills in English. If only part of one's identity is accepted, then we may only admit to that part of our identity, so for example, children may be uncertain whether to describe themselves as Punjabi or English speaking. The acceptance by people of an individual's identity can be on differing levels. Aspects of cultural life, such as wearing a turban and eating curried food may be accepted but the colour of a person's skin may be the cause of discrimination. The physically disabled child in a mainstream school can be accepted in many ways but is always seen as lacking in the aspect of the labelled disability and is therefore identified by deficiency. This then becomes the overriding aspect that signifies their identity. As teachers we have a responsibility to recognize the special needs of the children in our care. But the dilemma is when identifying a particular aspect, we label the whole child as deficient. The term 'special needs' conveys negative and discriminatory boundaries between the 'normal' and the 'not normal' (Taylor and Costley 1995) The same is true for the term 'ethnic minority' as this also conveys a sense of inequality with the majority. We need to get away from the deficit aspect of identifying needs and look for the positive elements of the difference. If we do not differentiate then we 'treat them all the same' but this blind approach implies that we pursue strategies that normalize rather than acknowledge creative individuality and diversity (Cornwall 1996). Instead of looking for conformity, we should treat people equally by celebrating the diversity.

Children and teachers have a responsibility to their own community to acknowledge their membership, even if this is held in low esteem by the school or wider society. But being overtly proud of our background can be seen as over asserting our self-image. For example, declaring at every opportunity, that 'I am working class', 'I'm a Northerner' or 'I am a committed Christian' puts down a marker for others' response and can close doors. There may be a need to assert oneself to cover a feeling of inadequacy. Respect and acknowledgement should come from one's behaviour not identity label and people should be in a climate where they have the choice of how to identify themselves.

Life in a culturally diverse society is not static but dynamic (Modood *et al.* 1994; Gaine 1995). The development of global communications has influenced fashion, music, food tastes and political ideas. The images children see on television and the food that is available to most families reflect a multi-ethnic world and bring changes for minority cultures as well as for the indigenous majority. Especially in areas of high ethnic minority population, a culture has developed that is influenced by the majority lifestyle but rooted in the minority. The host language English is mixed with the heritage language, for example a sentence in a south Asian language will be peppered with English words and idioms. This 'language switching' is a common occurrence (Whitehead 1996b). Children will try to be part of both traditions and attempt to find a new image. This can produce conflict for the young who are perceived to be abandoning their heritage in favour of Western ways. But is this any different from the generation gap found in every culture? As teachers, we must be aware of the complexity of identity and the pressures on young children. This means acknowledging the lifestyle led by each individual child and emphasizing the common strands shared by children and adults living together in Britain.

## Educational responsibilities within a political context

We believe that it is the school's responsibility to provide an environment of safety for children. To ensure that this is achieved, we must not only consider the physical aspects of a secure environment but children's social and emotional safety. Finding ways to narrow the gap between the rhetoric of addressing inequality and the reality of classroom practice should be considered a prime responsibility by all those involved in education. Cole (1997) argues that a commitment to 'equality' means going further than promoting equal opportunity policies. It means challenging the inequalities that are found in the structures in education and the wider society. How much schools should address questions such as whether they reinforce the class structure of society or whether it is their responsibility to try and change it are matters of public debate. But when as teachers we find ourselves having to justify educational practice in a political context, as the teacher had to do in cameo 1, we are faced with dilemmas. We have been castigated for taking up issues, for example, by John Major when he spoke at the 1992 Conservative Party Conference: 'Primary teachers should teach children to read, not waste their time on the politics of gender, race and class.'

Schools have got to operate within political constraints and are accountable to governing bodies. An example of how teachers and schools respond to the political context would be the response to the published league tables of SATs results. If the tables show a village school with 100 per cent of the children entered gaining Level 4 in the Key Stage 2 SATs then this can result in house prices rising in the village as everyone with young children wishes to live there. The pressure on the school to provide 100 per cent results every year will be enormous. But what of the inner city school at the bottom of the table? Teachers here may strongly believe in equal opportunities and so they include all children in all aspects of the tests whereas the village school may not enter an expected failure. These are the educational choices made by teachers in the political context.

In many of the documents produced from central government, the rhetoric of addressing equality issues can be found but the reality, in terms of classroom practice, is sadly lacking. The working parties devising the National Curriculum at the end of the 1980s, were instructed to take account of the ethnic and cultural diversity of British society and to promote equal opportunities for all (Tomlinson 1991). The actual content of the curriculum in terms of meeting this requirement has been widely criticized (Tomlinson 1991; Troyna and Hatcher 1992). White (1987) states that the values underlying the curriculum were taken as read by central government and the curriculum prescribed on that basis. The Runnymede Trust studied Ofsted inspection reports and found them lacking in emphasizing improvements regarding equality issues (Runnymede Trust 1995). In the area of teacher training, Hill (1994) states that the competencies expected of Newly Qualified Teachers (as set out in DES Circular 14/93) contain no explicit reference to recognizing or responding to forms of inequality. These were the forerunner of the standards for the award of Qualified Teacher Status (Teacher Training Agency 1997) which state that new teachers should ensure that all children are given the opportunity to achieve their potential. The demonstration of whether a student teacher has fulfilled this requirement or not is open to wide interpretation by both the student, the training institution and schools. The responsibility for teachers to respond to issues of inequality is, once again, left open to each individual.

The reduction of the power and influence of Local Education Authorities (Troyna 1995) has resulted in the frameworks constructed for antiracist policies to be dismantled. But, as Klein and

Siraj-Blatchford (1991) state, the promotion of race equality (and other inequalities) has been dropped from the agenda of government and many local education authorities. Policy determination is now in the hands of governing bodies and the attitudes of the most dominant members will be influential. We ask whether one isolated ethnic minority governor or a few women surrounded by a majority of 'grey-suited' governors from the business sector, can hope to influence policies towards a strong stance on equality issues?

Cortazzi (1991), drawing on accounts by primary teachers about their teaching experiences, found that the social context of primary education was frequently referred to but not the political context. It can be conjectured that this emphasis results in teachers identifying the cause of the educational problems as children's backgrounds rather than as political factors. So families are blamed and the structures and attitudes of society are not considered. If teachers examine the political context, they may hold a more positive view of the social context and, instead of concentrating on identifying problems, they might then be in a position to place more emphasis on adjusting the educational context to improve children's learning opportunities.

Most schools have an equal opportunity policy so staff feel that the issue has been addressed, but the reality in the classroom is different. Research carried out by Ofsted (1996a: 55) showed a 'considerable gulf between the daily reality experienced by black pupils and the stated goal of equal opportunities for all'. So what can the individual teacher do? Children are in school for less than 20 per cent of their waking hours (Alexander 1997) so the role of the school needs to be kept in perspective. The individual teacher's influence will be in the day-to-day interactions with children. As teachers, it is our responsibility to be informed and to use our knowledge to make decisions in the best interests of the children. This should be both from the short term perspective of immediate need and in the long term interests of social justice for all.

Society holds expectations that teachers will deliver a high level of academic achievement. But there are so many influences on primary education that often teachers feel they personally have little control. To help you explore this issue in the context of your school, try answering the following questions.

---

**ACTIVITY 6.1**

Influences

In your school, who has the most influence? Try completing
Table 6.1.
   After doing this activity, you may feel that an individual
teacher does not have very much control but it is the day-to-day
interactions between child and teacher that matter most. As
we have explored earlier in this book, the relationships with
children, the mode of communication and the environment
provided for learning are the responsibility of the individual
teacher. Choices are therefore made by the teacher using
considerable professional knowledge and skill.

---

## Use of terminology

Ideas about nomenclature for different groups of people are
constantly shifting and it is therefore difficult to keep up with
the current terminology and, most importantly, to understand
the reasons that underlie any changes. Decisions on whether or
not to use 'politically correct' terminology can cause concerns for
some teachers. There has been a swing of the pendulum in public
opinion from attacks on people for insensitive use of descriptive
words to attacks for being too politically correct. But issues of
nomenclature are a serious issue and have been trivialized by the
media. Insensitive use of language can be damaging to children
(Cornwall 1996).
   To address this issue in terms of our relationships with children and adults in primary education, we suggest that it should
be like climbing a ladder. You may need to take each rung one at
a time to feel comfortable with using terminology that does not
offend. It is important to examine exactly what the terminology
means in any specific context. Different people may have different interpretations depending on their previous experiences.
Shared understanding of meaning is important so that people do
not feel threatened. Not to express something maybe a sign of
progression for it shows the individual is sufficiently aware to
know that it would be unsuitable to express a view, so they keep

Table 6.1

| | Class teacher | Government | Local education authority | School management | Parent | Children | Local community | Other |
|---|---|---|---|---|---|---|---|---|
| Content of the curriculum | | | | | | | | |
| Day-to-day content of the children's learning | | | | | | | | |
| Mode of delivery | | | | | | | | |
| Classroom organization | | | | | | | | |
| Method of assessment | | | | | | | | |
| Use of assessments | | | | | | | | |
| Classroom rules | | | | | | | | |
| Punishments | | | | | | | | |
| Resources | | | | | | | | |
| Content of displays | | | | | | | | |

it to themselves. For example, how might you describe children where one parent is of white European origin and one parent is of black African origin? The following suggestions (Davis and Evans 1997) show the changes in acceptable terminology and the progression of ideas.

| | |
|---|---|
| *Half caste* | A derogatory term used in the past with colonial connotations. |
| *Half white* | Ignores the black. |
| *Half black* | Ignores the white. |
| *Mixed race* | Only refers to race and does not take account of same race parents with different cultures, religions or modes of communication. |
| *Bicultural* | Only refers to culture not ethnicity if the family follows a mainly British culture. |
| *Dual heritage* | Celebration of duality. This can be applied to any child where the parents' backgrounds have significant differences and therefore affect the child's sense of identity. |

We would strongly agree with Davis and Evans (1997) that individuals should have the right to decide what to call themselves. A climate must be created which allows a child to come to recognize their own identity for themselves and to define it. This climate must be a non-judgemental one in which the child can learn about both backgrounds and how these relate to the experience of living in Britain.

Although the political context is influential, teachers, like other professionals, have to continue to perform the task as well as they are able, and it is certainly to teachers' credit that although policies may change, sometimes quite rapidly, they achieve a high standard of performance in a conscientious way. Being resourceful whatever the circumstances, teachers have carried on working hard, even though their value in the perception of society has diminished. Teachers have carried on valuing children, because they are working for children. The effect that we as teachers have on children by providing a role model is the vital factor. If we model respect for all people and demonstrate that we value diversity, then children will absorb these messages and hopefully demonstrate the same consideration themselves. The only way that teachers will be able to move forward is to be informed, to have knowledge, to be able to keep going with the system. At the end of the day, it is teachers who hold the crucial knowledge. It is we who must provide, for those who hold positions of authority, information concerning the relationships systems which work and which do not.

## Strategies for finding commonality while respecting difference

Swann (1985: 5) referring to the education of ethnic minority children, suggests that children should be brought up 'within a framework of commonly accepted values, practices and procedures' whilst allowing communities to maintain distinct identities within this common framework.

The crucial words in this statement are 'maintain distinct identities' and 'common framework'. As we have indicated throughout this book, reference to ethnic minorities can be substituted to encompass all forms of diversity. The issue to be addressed by all in education is how these two ideals can co-exist. We have argued that individual children's and teacher's distinct identities should be acknowledged and we have tried to provide a rationale why this is important in primary education. We will now explore how these can be maintained within the common framework. The key to valuing diversity is to establish commonly accepted practices and procedures as advocated by Swann (1985) within a framework of commonly accepted values.

## Does multicultural education create differences?

It is sometimes argued that providing multicultural activities, which give children knowledge of diverse lifestyles, only emphasizes the differences between people. But children are not always conscious of being part of a distinct culture because their way of life is the natural one for them. It is only when they encounter different ways that they can make comparisons. This is why it is so important that when children encounter a variety of lifestyles, they recognize that their own is valued. No child should be made to feel that their home life is inadequate. The commonalities between experiences must be explored and given emphasis.

Another argument frequently used against the acknowledgement of diversity, is that by pointing out ethnic differences one
might exacerbate racism (Hatcher *et al.* 1996). But if we adopt a
'colour blind' approach we deny a person's identity. As one child
was heard to say: 'If you don't see me as black, do you see me at
all?' It is the response to the 'colour', or any other aspect of difference such as disability, that is at issue. If all elements of a child's
identity are celebrated, then acknowledging difference will not
create problems. We cannot make a person's identity null and
void as it is constantly maintained in that individual's behaviour
patterns and thinking processes.

### From rhetoric to practice

Primary education should be about individuals realizing their
full potential through a wide curriculum and an acknowledgement of diversity. A child will only be able to relate to aspects of
curriculum as long as there is a positive self-image in place, and
we can only have a positive self-image by acknowledging diversity: every child is different from every other. But can this ideal
work in a class of over 30, mixed ability, Year 3 or 4 children? This
is when the rhetoric has to become reality as the National Curriculum requirements have to be put in place. We need to look at
the way we interpret the programmes of study to allow for the
acknowledgement of diversity. The approach to lesson planning
is crucial here. Differentiation is already included in teacher's
planning in terms of children's abilities in skills, topic knowledge
and concepts. But it is also necessary to take account of children's diverse backgrounds and the impact of these on their learning. Differentiation may be planned for the outcome of what the
children do or in the actual task set. The following is a practical
example of this approach.

---

**STRATEGY**

**Commonality respecting differences**

We will consider a creative writing lesson on 'celebrations' with
a class of Key Stage 2 children. The class includes a boy from
a Jehovah's Witness background. One aspect of diversity for

followers of that faith is that they do not celebrate birthdays or Christmas. So when planning the lesson, the question to be raised is whether that child carries out the task or whether an alternative should be found. The answer must be for him to participate in the set activity because the writing would provide an opportunity for the expression of views on why he does not celebrate birthdays. His views and opinions are just as valid as those of the other children. Also, one of the lesson aims would be to develop the communication of ideas to others. The child from the Jehovah's Witness family can write descriptions of how they acknowledge the passing of each year, and why they do not celebrate birthday or Christmas. He will be giving reasons for his belief, which will extend the other children's experiences. All the class will have commonality in the writing task about their own experiences but the outcome will be differentiated.

## STRATEGY

### 'What did you have for breakfast?' Lesson example

A further example of how we can plan for diversity while emphasizing the commonality of children's experiences would be the following lesson on 'Breakfast'.

*The aims*

The lesson aims:

- for children to understand that food is needed for energy and growth;
- for children to understand that a varied diet is essential to health;
- to introduce children to the use of grains as a basic food material;
- to provide knowledge of how other children live and for diversity to be accepted and commonality found.

*The task*

Children describe the breakfast eaten that morning first to a partner and then to a group. Working collaboratively, they classify the different food items eaten by the group members by contents, i.e. grains, meat, dairy, fruit. Children present this on a large sheet of paper.

*The method*

Our knowledge of the children can influence the organization of groupings. For example, if we are aware that there are children who will not have had breakfast at all then we can place them sensitively and encourage them to describe the occasion of their first food of the day. They might not have eaten until consuming a packet of crisps at breaktime, but you can still explain what breakfast means – 'breaking the night's fast'. In this way you will not be presenting a value judgement or describing only one way of living as an acceptable norm. The task will also provide an opportunity for children to describe who made the breakfast and where they eat it. This will encourage discussion of gender issues.

*The discussion*

In discussion at the end of the lesson, it can be pointed out that there is diversity in grains, which produces the diversity in cereals, on the breakfast table, which then allows diversity in choice of what and how to eat. The fact that two children have had chapattis is no greater difference than the one child who has had 'Shredded Wheat' or a boiled egg. We must be careful not to isolate any child but to maintain that the commonality among the class is the food that they have had for breakfast. Also, children will not have a totally English breakfast or perhaps a totally Asian one but a combination of food types. This will show children that cultures are dynamic and that all are influenced by fashion and marketing.

## Finding the common framework

As we have previously stated, determining the common framework is complex. It cannot be assumed that society as a mass has a common value system. The cultural diversity present in British society today has given rise to 'complex contrasting value systems within which schools and teachers must try to operate' (Galton 1995: 4). The following statement was referring to ethnic minorities but is equally true for children growing up in a defined class structure or religious family:

> Young people have to contend not only with the Babel of values in the wider society, but also with the rift between that Babel and the traditional values of their own community.
>
> (White 1987: 16)

But for a school to carry out its responsibility to provide children with a set of common values to uphold is immensely difficult. We refer back to the notion of the insurance policy (see p. 103), which protects our valuable possessions, and we suggest that it is imperative that all schools try to agree on the items to be insured.

In an editorial in the *Guardian* (1996) regarding the role of the school in guarding the nation's moral values, it was stated 'the first goal of every school should be an explicit statement on the values that guide its practice'. There will be as many ways to carry this out as there will be schools but an attempt at a whole-school approach to finding common values should be made. The aims of the school should be defined in terms of the purposes of the education provided and the methods used to achieve the purpose. These aims would then provide a framework that can be monitored and evaluated. Statements alone are just rhetoric if there is no system to monitor the practice.

Pollard (1985) suggests that the school climate is likely to reflect the perspectives of those with most power and influence in the school. The challenge for school managers is to use their power to ensure that those without official status do have some influence on the ethos of the school. We would suggest adopting the 'large table approach' suggested in Chapter 5 (see page 83). There will be a need for careful chairing of the discussion to ensure participation for all and to achieve an outcome. Participants will bring understandings of gender, cultural and disability issues that can enhance the knowledge of others.

## Whole-school conference

As many of the people who are concerned for the welfare of the school should be involved in discussions. Methods could be devised to have small group discussions followed by delegates at a final conference. This would ensure that parents, governors, lunchtime, clerical and support staff have a voice. The ideas of the children should not be forgotten!

### Step one

Produce definitions that have consensus (not everyone is going to agree with every word used). It is best to start with ones where there is general agreement. Try this statement as a first attempt.

There should be an attractive working environment in the school.

## Step two

Try more complex and potentially contentious statements. Remember, as Cole (1997) states, it is easier to establish terms that are not acceptable than to find ones that all agree with. The following statement by Gillborn (1990) would spark debate.

Education is not a competition but an attempt to give the best support and opportunities for all groups.

## Step three

Examine the practical application for each statement. All who must carry out the day-to-day activities in the school must understand the implications for each issue.

A 'large table approach' can bring agreement across communities but making sure that ownership of the final statements is felt by all is especially vital for the success of the exercise.

## Step four

Communicate to all involved in the school when there is an agreed set of common values that underpin the education conducted in the school. Don't forget to include the children.

## Step five

Establish a method of monitoring and evaluating the various aspects of school life to ensure that these accord with the agreed values.

## Conclusion

This book has tried to extend the discussion about equal opportunities in primary education. We have moved away from single issues such as race and gender and given recognition to the interface of different aspects of identity that make up individual children and individual teachers. The examples used are from real primary school life as only in this way will we relate to real primary teachers teaching in real schools.

We have not suggested that it will be easy but as Klein (1997: 17) writes: 'Only by zero tolerance of inequality can quality improve for all children.' We want all people with responsibility for the education of the young to see how their attitudes influence the actions that are taken in the classroom and beyond. It is the influence upon the educational process that is important. Let us aim to provide a quality built 'store cupboard' where children, teachers and everyone concerned with primary education, can have open access to the brightly displayed, valuable items on the shelves. Let us create an environment where no one feels that any item must be hidden away and all can find commonality and celebrate the diversity.

Now for story time.

# Epilogue

Like all good primary teachers, we will bring the learning to a close with a story.

The scenario is that of a young student, Meena, training to be a primary school teacher and placed in an inner-city school for a teaching practice. Nothing at all unusual! She is of Asian origin and the majority of the pupils, together with a considerable number of the staff, are likewise of Asian background. The school has been conscientious in fulfilling its role of providing the children with a wealth of experiences and, indeed, a warm environment to celebrate and promote their cultural backgrounds. Staff are proud of their first languages and their heritage. There is therefore a recognition and expression of diversity in a hundred ways.

What could be more natural therefore than a friendly child saying to the new teacher, તમે કયાં રહો છો?

Meena is both surprised and confused. Why, you may well ask? The answer, surprisingly, is that she cannot understand what the child has said. But why should we be surprised? Culture is above all fluid. It does not stay at one spot nor can we easily predict its path. Meena has come from a home where it was acknowledged that the mastery of the English language was seen as a priority in order to progress up both the social and professional ladder. The corollary of that has been a 'watering down' of some aspects of the cultural heritage. This has included less and less use of the original mother tongue so that by the time of this particular young persons's generation it is spoken hardly at all. The same thing may be equally true of other aspects of the original culture.

For Meena there is most certainly an initial culture shock. She is a member of staff in a school where the value of a wide variety of first languages is given a prominent position. Assemblies celebrating festivals of a similarly wide range is a familiar experience for staff and pupils, and must, necessarily at times, occupy substantial parts of the school day. This ethos is directly opposite to that which has moulded her own set of values. Moreover, she has a strange feeling of inadequacy for not only is she unable to participate in communications which do not rely on English, but it may be that she is also not so familiar with cultural practices of which the children and other staff have considerable knowledge. Her Eurocentric view is challenged by all that are around her, just at the time when she has a need for respect from both children and colleagues.

But at the centre of the incident is a child fully confident in the value of his home culture. His school both acknowledges and encourages everything from his home and community background which has defined his identity. He is a developing bilingual and can happily transfer from one language to another with a gradually increasing accuracy. It was perfectly natural for him to address a teacher with an Asian appearance in his first language. He was surprised – perhaps shocked – when she was unable to understand him and therefore unable to respond.

What has really happened is that both child and student have had stereotypes challenged. The student assumed that the aim of 'good education' was to Anglicize the process to an extreme degree. The child assumed that an Asian face denoted a strongly Asian background in a traditional form.

Both of these individuals are operating within the same environment. The school has carefully created an ethos which values the diversity of its pupils. The awareness of the issues involved has been raised over a number of years and full use has been made of local and national training initiatives. It is a school to be visited and presents a challenging image for others to follow. But what of the discrepancy, very much in evidence between the position of the student teacher and the child? What has gone wrong? The answer is 'nothing'. The real question is: 'What has happened?' The answer to that question is that the school has tackled the issues concerning diversity successfully, but has travelled only some distance along the line. It must now address the further challenge of the mobility of culture and the diversities within that. Because of this mobility, any community is somewhere on a scale which embraces the traditional and the most modern approach that we can imagine. A community or family or individual, can be at any point on that scale, and may also move to and fro on it continually. There are no set points upon which someone stays. It is rather a state of constant fluidity.

Furthermore, it is the responsibility of everyone of us to respect an individual's right to decide where on that scale he or she wishes to stand. Thereby we truly promote diversity.

# References

Abbott, D. (1996) Teachers and pupils: expectations and judgements, in P. Croll (ed.) *Teachers, Pupils and Primary Schooling*. London: Cassell.

Ainscow, M. and Muncey, J. (1989) *Meeting Individual Needs in the Primary School*. London: David Fulton.

Ackers, J. (1994) 'Why involve me?' Encouraging children and their parents to participate in the assessment process, in L. Abbott and R. Rodgers (eds) *Quality Education in the Early Years*. Buckingham: Open University Press.

Alexander, R. (1996) *Policy and Practice in Primary Education. Local Initiative, National Agenda*. London: Routledge.

Alexander, T. (1997) Learning begins at home. Implications for a learning society, in B. Cosin and M. Hales (eds) *Families, Education and Social Differences*. London: Routledge.

Antonouris, G. and Wilson, J. (1989) *Equal Opportunities in Schools*. London: Cassell.

Atkin, J. and Bastiani, J. with Goode, J. (1988) *Listening to Parents*. Beckenham: Croom Helm.

Ausubel, D. P., Novak, J. D. and Hanesian, H. (1978) *Educational Psychology: A Cognitive View*, 2nd edn. New York: Holt, Rinehart and Winston.

Ayles, R. (1996) Differentiation? Working with more able children. In P. Croll and N. Hastings (eds) *Effective Primary Teaching. Research-based Classroom Strategies*. London: David Fulton.

Ball, C. (1994) *Start Right: The Importance of Early Learning*. London: RSA.

Bastiani, J. (1997) *Home–School Work in Multicultural Settings*. London: David Fulton.

Beetlestone, F. (1998) *Creative Children: Imaginative Teaching*. Buckingham: Open University Press.

Bernstein, B. (1971) *Class, Codes and Control*. London: Routledge and Kegan Paul.

Biggs, J. B. (1994) What are effective schools? Lessons from East and West. *Australian Educational Researcher*, 21: 19–40.

Brice Heath, S. (1983) *Ways with Words*. Cambridge: Cambridge University Press.

Brophy, J. (1983) Research on the self-fulfilling prophecy and teacher expectations. *Journal of Educational Psychology*, 75(5): 631–66.

Brown, G. and Wragg, E. C. (1993) *Questioning*. London: Routledge.

Browne, N. and France, P. (1985) Only cissies wear dresses: a look at sexist talk in the nursery, in G. Weiner (ed.) *Just a Bunch of Girls*. Milton Keynes: Open University Press.

Bruner, J. (1996) *The Culture of Education*. Cambridge, MA: Harvard University Press.

Bullock Report (1975) *A Language for Life*. London: HMSO.

Burns, R. (1982) *Self-Concept Development and Education*. Eastbourne: Holt, Rinehart and Winston.

Calderhead, J. (1987) *Exploring Teachers' Thinking*. London: Cassell Educational.

Clark, C. and Peterson, P. (1986) Teachers' thought processes, in M. Wittrock (ed.) *Handbook of Research on Teaching*, 3rd edn. New York: Macmillan.

Cole, M. (1997) Equality and primary education: what are the conceptual issues?, in M. Cole, D. Hill and S. Shan (eds) *Promoting Equality in Primary School*. London: Cassell.

Connell, R., Ashenden, D., Kessler, S. and Dowsett, G. (1982) *Making the Difference: Schools, Families and Social Division*. Sydney: George Allen and Unwin.

Cornwall, J. (1996) in D. Hayes (ed.) *Debating Education. Issues for the New Millennium?* Canterbury: Christ Church College.

Cortazzi, M. (1991) *Primary Teaching. How It Is*. London: David Fulton.

Cummins, J. (1996) Negotiating identities in the classroom and society. *Multicultural Teaching*, 15(1): 7–11.

Curtis, A. (1994) Play in different cultures and different childhoods, in J. R. Moyles (ed.) *The Excellence of Play*. Buckingham: Open University Press.

*Daily Mail* (1996) 5-year-olds to get gay lessons, 2 March.

Davis, L. and Evans, R. (1997) Meeting the needs of dual heritage children, in J. Bastiani (ed.) *Home–School Work in Multicultural Settings*. London: David Fulton.

Day, C. (1993) Reflection: A necessary but not sufficient condition for professional development, *British Educational Research Journal*, 19(1): 83–94.

Department for Education (1993) Circular 14/93. *The Initial Training of Teachers*. London: HMSO.

Department of Health (1989) *The Children Act 1989: Guidance and Regulations*. London: HMSO.

Docking, J. (1996) *Managing Behaviour in the Primary School*. London: David Fulton.

Donaldson, M. (1978) *Children's Minds*. Glasgow: Fontana.

Edwards, A. and Knight, P. (1994) *Effective Early Years Education*. Buckingham: Open University Press.

Edwards, A. and Knight, P. (1997) Parents and professionals, in B. Cosin and M. Hales (eds) *Families, Education and Social Differences*. London: Routledge.

Elliott, J. (1991) *Action Research for Educational Change*. Buckingham: Open University Press.

Epstein, D. (1994) *Challenging Lesbian and Gay Inequalities in Education*. Buckingham: Open University Press.

Faltis, C. (1993) Building bridges between parents and the school, in O. Garcia and C. Baker (eds) *Policy and Practice in Bilingual Education: Extending the Foundations*. Clevedon: Multilingual Matters.

Ferris, A. (1997) Bridging the gap between home and school, in J. Bastiani (ed.) *Home–School Work in Multicultural Settings*. London: David Fulton.

Gaine, C. (1995) *Still No Problem Here*. Stoke on Trent: Trentham Books.

Galton, M. and Williamson, J. (1992) *Group Work in the Primary Classroom*. London: Routledge.

Galton, M. (1995) *Crisis in the Primary Classroom*. London: David Fulton.

Gillborn, D. (1990) *'Race', Ethnicity and Education*. London: Unwin Hyman.

Good, T. L. (1987) Two decades of research on teacher expectations. Findings and future directions. *Journal of Teacher Education*, 38(4): 32–47.

*Guardian* (1996) Editorial. *Teaching Moral Values*, 16 January.

Hall, E. and Hall, C. (1988) *Human Relations in Education*. London: Routledge.

Harding, J. and Meldon-Smith, L. (1996) *How to Make Observations and Assessments*. London: Hodder and Stoughton.

Hatcher, R., Troyna, B. and Gewirz, D. (1996) *Racial Equality and the Local Management of Schools. Warwick Papers on Educational Policy No. 8*. Stoke on Trent: Trentham Books.

Hill, D. (1994) Initial teacher education and ethnic diversity, in G. Verma and P. Pumfrey (eds) *Cross Curricular Contexts, Themes and Dimensions in Primary Schools*. London: Falmer Press.

Hughes, M. (1989) The child as learner: the contrasting views of development psychology and early education, in C. Desforges (ed.) *Early Childhood Education*. Edinburgh: British Journal of Educational Psychology.

Hughes, M. and Westgate, D. (1997) Assistants as talk-partners in early-years classrooms: some issues of support and development. *Educational Review*, 49(1): 5–12.

Johnson, G., Hill, B. and Tunstall, P. (1992) *Primary Records of Achievement: A Teacher's Guide to Reviewing, Recording and Reporting*. London:
Hodder and Stoughton.

King, R. (1978) *All Things Bright and Beautiful*. London: John Wiley.

Kitson, N. (1994) 'Please Miss Alexander, will you be the robber?' Fant-
asy play: a case for adult intervention, in J. R. Moyles (ed.) *The Excellence of Play*. Buckingham: Open University Press.

Klein, G. (1997) Excellence . . . but for whom? *The Guardian*, 12 August.

Klein, G. and Siraj-Blatchford, I. (1991) National Conference on 'Entitlement for All?' Race, Gender and the ERA. *Multicultural Teaching to
Combat Racism in School and Community*, 10(1): 3–4.

Kutnick, P. J. (1988) *Relationships in the Primary Classroom*. London: Paul
Chapman.

Lawrence, D. (1996) *Enhancing Self Esteem in the Classroom*, 2nd edn.
London: Paul Chapman.

Lewis, M. and Kellaghan, T. (1993) *Exploring the Gender Gap in Primary
Schools*. Dublin: Educational Research Centre, St Patrick's College.

Mac an Ghaill, M. (1995) *The Making of Men. Masculinities, Sexualities and
Schooling*. Buckingham: Open University Press.

Major, J. (1992) 'Leader's speech' to Conservative Party Conference,
October.

Marshall, G., Rose, D., Newby, H. and Vogler, C. (1989) *Social Class in
Modern Britain*. London: Unwin Hyman.

McNamara, S. (1995) Let's co-operate! Developing children's social skills
in the Classroom, in J. R. Moyles (ed.) *Beginning Teaching, Beginning
Learning*. Buckingham: Open University Press.

McNamara, S. and Moreton, G. (1995) *Changing Behaviour. Teaching Children with Emotional and Behavioural Difficulties in Primary and Secondary
Classrooms*. London: David Fulton.

Merry, R. (1998) *Successful Children, Successful Teaching*. Buckingham: Open
University Press.

Modood, T., Berishan, S. and Virdee, S. (1994) *Changing Ethnic Identities*,
London: Policy Studies Institute.

Mooney, T. (1995) Prejudice is in the hands of the beholder. *Times Educational Supplement*, 1 September.

Morgan, V. and Dunn, S. (1988) Chameleons in the classroom: visible
and invisible children in nursery and infant classrooms. *Educational
Review*, 40(1): 3–12.

Mortimore, P., Sammons, P., Stoll, L., Lewis, D. and Ecob, R. (1988)
*School Matters: The Junior Years*. Wells: Open Books.

Moyles J. (1989) *Just Playing*. Milton Keynes: Open University Press.

Moyles J. (1992) *Organising for Learning in the Primary Classroom*. Buckingham: Open University Press.

Moyles J. and Suschitzky, W. (1994) A survey of nursery teachers and
nursery nurses in Leicestershire, unpublished research.

Moyles J. with Suschitzky, W. (1997a) *Jills of All Trades. Classroom Assistants in KS1 Classes.* Leicester: Association of Teachers and Lecturers with Leicester University.

Moyles J. with Suschitzky, W. (1997b) *The Buck Stops Here. Nursery Teachers and Nursery Nurses Working Together.* Leicester: University of Leicester.

Nias, J. (1989) *Primary Teachers Talking.* London: Routledge.

Norman, K. (1990) *Teaching Talking and Learning in Key Stage One: A booklet for teachers based on the work of the National Oracy Project.* York: National Curriculum Council.

Oakley, A. (1985) *Sex, Gender and Society.* Aldershot: Gower.

Ofsted (1995) *Reporting Pupils' Achievements.* London: HMSO.

Ofsted (1996a) *Recent Research on the Achievement of Ethnic Minority Pupils.* London: HMSO.

Ofsted (1996b) *Standards and Quality in Education 1994/5. Annual Report of Her Majesty's Chief Inspector of Schools.* London: HMSO.

Ogilvy, C., Boath, E., Cheyne, W., Jahoda, G. and Schaffer, R. (1990) Staff attitudes and perceptions in multi-cultural nursery schools. *Early Child Development and Care,* 64: 1–13.

Pattanyak, D. (1981) *Multilingualism and Mother Tongue Education.* Oxford: Oxford University Press.

Pollard, A. (1985) *The Social World of the Primary School.* London: Cassell.

Pollard, A. (1996) *The Social World of Children's Learning.* London: Cassell.

Pring, R. (1992) Education for a pluralist society, in M. Leicester and M. Taylor (eds) *Ethics, Ethnicity and Education.* London: Kogan Page.

Ritchie, R. (1991) *Profiling in Primary schools: A Handbook for Teachers.* London: Cassell.

Rogers, C. (1982) *A Social Psychology of Schooling.* London: Routledge and Kegan Paul.

Rosenthal, R. and Jacobson, L. (1968) *Pygmalion in the Classroom.* New York: Holt, Rinehart and Winston.

Runnymede Trust, (1995) *Equal Opportunities and the Inspection of Schools: A Statement of Concern.* London: Runnymead Trust.

Salmon, P. (1988) *Psychology for Teachers.* London: Hutchinson.

Schmid, J. (1961) Factor analysis of the teaching complex. *Journal of Experimental Education,* 30(1): 58.

Siraj-Blatchford, I. (1994) *The Early Years, Laying the Foundations for Racial Equality.* Stoke on Trent: Trentham Books.

Siraj-Blatchford, I. (1995) Racial equality education: identity, curriculum and pedagogy, in J. Siraj-Blatchford and I. Siraj-Blatchford (eds) *Educating the Whole Child.* Buckingham: Open University Press.

Smith, P. and Cowie, H. (1991) *Understanding Children's Development.* Oxford: Blackwell.

Stammers, P. (1992) The Greeks had a word for it. *British Journal of In-Service Education,* 18(2): 76–80.

Suschitzky, W. (1995a) Equal opportunities in practice, in J. R. Moyles (ed.) *Beginning Teaching, Beginning Learning*. Buckingham: Open University Press.

Suschitzky, W. (1995b) Cross-Cultural Mentoring, unpublished MA dissertation, University of Leicester.

Swadener, E. and Johnson, J. (1989) Play in diverse social contexts: parent and teacher roles, in M. Bloch and A. Pellegrini (eds) *The Ecological Context of Children's Play*. New York: Ablex.

Swann Report (1985) *Education For All*. London: HMSO.

Taylor, A. S. and Costley, D. (1995) Effective schooling for all: the 'special educational needs', in J. Siraj-Blatchford and I. Siraj-Blatchford (eds) *Educating the Whole Child*. Buckingham: Open University Press.

Teacher Training Agency (1997) *Career Entry Profile. Standards for the Award of Qualified Teacher Status*. London: Teacher Training Agency.

Thomas, N. (1985) *The Thomas Report – Improving Primary Schools*. London: Inner London Education Authority.

Tiedt, P. and Tiedt, I. (1990) *Multicultural Teaching*. Boston, MA: Allyn and Bacon.

Tomlinson, S. (1991) The National Curriculum and the multicultural dimension. *New Community*, 17(3): 434–40.

Tough, J. (1977) *The Development of Meaning: A Study of Children's Use of Language*. London: Allen and Unwin.

Troyna, B. (1995) The local management of schools and racial equality, in S. Tomlinson and M. Craft (eds) *Ethnic Relations and Schooling*. London: Athlone.

Troyna, B. and Hatcher, R. (1992) *Racism in Children's Lives. A Study of Mainly-White Primary Schools*. London: Routledge.

Vasconcelos, T. (1997) Planting the field of Portuguese preschool education: old roots and new policies. *European Early Childhood Education Research Journal*, 5(1): 5–16.

Verma, G. (1988) Issues in multicultural education, in G. Verma and P. Pumfrey (eds) *Educational Attainments. Issues and Outcomes in Multicultural Education*. Lewes: Falmer Press.

Verma, G. and Mallick, K. (1988) Self-esteem and educational achievement in British young South Asians, in G. Verma and P. Pumfrey (eds) *Educational Attainments. Issues and Outcomes in Multicultural Education*. Lewes: Falmer Press.

Weinstein, R. (1983) Student perceptions of schooling. *Elementary School Journal*, 83: 287–312.

Wells, G. (1987) *The Meaning Makers. Children Learning Language and Using Language to Learn*. Sevenoaks: Hodder and Stoughton.

Wells, G. (1992) The centrality of talk in education, in K. Norman (ed.) *Thinking Voices: The Work of the National Oracy Project*. London: Hodder and Stoughton.

White, J. (1987) The quest for common values, in G. Haydon (ed.) *Education for a Pluralist Society*. London: University of London.

Whitehead, M. (1996a) New attempt to promote lessons in gay tolerance. *Times Educational Supplement*, 1 March.

Whitehead, M. R. (1996b) *The Development of Language and Literacy*. London: Hodder and Stoughton.

Whitehead, M. R. (1998) *Language and Literacy in the Early Years*, 2nd edn. London: Paul Chapman.

Wolfendale, S. (1992) *Empowering Parents and Teachers*. London: Cassell.

Wolfendale, S. and Topping, K. (1996) *Family Involvement in Literacy. Effective Partners in Education*. London: Cassell.

Wood, D. (1988) *How Children Think and Learn: The Social Contexts of Cognitive Development*. Oxford: Blackwell.

Wood, M. (1997) Home–school work with traveller children and their families, in J. Bastiani (ed.) *Home–School Work in Multicultural Settings*. London: David Fulton.

Woods, P. (1990) *The Happiest Days? How Pupils Cope with School*. Basingstoke: Falmer Press.

Wragg, E. (1991) *The Leverhulme Primary Project*. Exeter: University of Exeter.

# Index

## EDUCATING THE WHOLE CHILD
CROSS-CURRICULAR SKILLS, THEMES AND DIMENSIONS

### John and Iram Siraj-Blatchford (eds)

This book approaches the 'delivery' of the cross-curricular skills, themes and dimensions from a perspective emphasizing the culture of primary schools and the social worlds of children. The authors argue that the teaching of skills, attitudes, concepts and knowledge to young children should not be seen as separate or alternative objectives, but rather as complementary and essential elements of the educational process. It is the teacher's role to help children develop and build upon the understandings, skills, knowledge and attitudes which they bring with them into school. Learning for young children is a social activity where new skills and understandings are gained through interaction with both adults and with their peers. Each of the approaches outlined in the book is thus grounded in an essential respect and empathy for children and childhood as a distinct stage in life and not merely a preparation for the world of adulthood. For instance, the authors argue that responsibilities and decision-making are everyday experiences for children and that they need to be able to develop attitudes and skills which enable them to participate fully in their own social world.

### Contents

### Contributors

John Bennett, Debra Costley, Debbie Epstein, Peter Lang, Val Millman, Lina Patel, Alistair Ross, Ann Sinclair Taylor, Iram Siraj-Baltchford, John Siraj-Blatchford, Balbir Kaur Sohal, Janice Wale.

192pp    0 335 19444 3 (paperback)    0 335 19445 1 (hardback)